DECEPTIONS AND BETRAYALS

Enjoy!

Mattie Westra

DECEPTIONS AND BETRAYALS

Marty Wurtz

ISBN : 1-4196-4678-8
Library of Congress Control Number : 2006907851

To order additional copies, please contact us.
BookSurge, LLC
www.booksurge.com
1-866-308-6235
orders@booksurge.com

DECEPTIONS AND BETRAYALS

I dedicate this book to my husband, Frank—the love of my life, my best friend, and my soul mate.

As we have said many times over the years, we can survive anything as long as we have each other and God guiding our way!

CHAPTER ONE

It was a beautiful sunny day, highly unusual for February in Trousdale, Kansas. The little red brick church was packed with an overflow of mourners outside. Merab had passed away, leaving her husband, Howard, and four small children. Catherine, Merab's sister, took the baby home with her after the service. She had all four children, in addition to her own three, for the two weeks Merab was in the hospital for the surgery that took her life. When Howard called Catherine to tell her Merab was gone, he told her, "Don't tell the kiddies, I want to tell them myself." Howard was totally grief-stricken. He had lost the love of his life.

Merab's family thought they were going to step in to decide the fate of the four children and had them all going in different directions. Delorse, the oldest at eleven, was going to her Grandma Salser, who was a bitch. Laura, nine years old, was going to her Uncle Alden and Aunt Elsie. Uncle Alden, Merab's brother, was a stuffed shirt. Byron, who was seven years old, was going to Uncle Guy and Aunt Lula. He was getting the best deal of them all; Aunt Lula was Howard's sister. Martha, at twenty months old, was going to stay with Uncle Elmer and Aunt Catherine. They went to see an attorney, but didn't get to first base. The attorney was appalled. He said, "Before you waste a lot of my time and yours, these are the bare facts: You wouldn't have a leg to stand on since Howard is not a woman-chaser or a drunkard. Leave this family alone!"

After the funeral, Martha stayed with Uncle Elmer and Aunt Catherine during the week. Every weekend, Howard picked up the baby and took her home. After several weeks of this, Howard went out to their farm one Friday night to get Martha and Elmer met him as he was getting out of the car. In his normal belligerent tone, Elmer said to Howard, "You are not taking Martha home anymore! Every Sunday night you bring her back here and it takes us several days to settle her down again. Then on Friday night, here you come to take her again, for us to start all over Sunday night. You can come out anytime to see her, but from now on, she stays here." Howard stood there, face-to-face with his brother-in-law and exploded! You could have heard him for two country miles! "Martha is my daughter, and you or no one else is going to tell me what I can or can't do with her!" Howard charged into the house, grabbed Martha up in his arms, and at the same time announced to Catherine, "Get her clothes; I won't be bringing her back!"

The year was 1944 and World War II was still going strong. Howard was the janitor of the school and took Martha with him to work instead of hiring a babysitter when the older kids were in school. One of the teachers set up a crib in the back of her classroom. Every afternoon, she found Howard and took Martha to put her down for a nap in the crib. After school, the older children helped Howard dust mop all the hardwood floors in the school, in addition to their chores at home.

Elmer and his family were the upper crust of the community. He took over several farms during the great Depression by paying the delinquent taxes. Merab's parents were also well off financially. Merab graduated from college in 1931 at Emporia State University during the most difficult time of the Depression. She was a beautiful girl, inside as well as out, classy and well mannered; a real lady.

Elmer went to see his brother-in-law, Alden, and said, "What Merab saw in Howard is beyond me. He hasn't got an ounce of class and will never amount to a hill of beans. I'll talk to my buddy on the draft board and get him drafted." Someone on the draft board was fully aware of the situation and sent a telegram to the Department of Defense in Washington, D.C. The reply was, "Hands off! This man is needed at home more than we need him overseas, a widower with four small children!"

Elmer would not give up, and went to see his friends on the school board. If Howard lost his job, he would have to give up the children. During the ten years Howard had been the janitor; he not only kept the school clean—they had not hired a painter, plumber, or electrician. He did it all and kept everything in tip top shape, but was fired nevertheless.

Howard was devastated! He had no idea what he was going to do, with four little mouths to feed and no job. He thought, "If I worked for myself, I would never be in this situation again." Electricity was something that fascinated him. He studied text books day and night to learn more about the electrician trade. Money was tight, but the family had enough to eat; that was the important thing.

World War II was over and the whole country was booming, with guys and gals in the military coming home from overseas. Many farms across several counties had no electricity and the power company was adding high lines throughout the countryside. Howard past his tests with flying colors and received his license. He was now a professional electrician with his own business, *Stilts Electric*. He had a lot of the tools needed to get started, and set up an account with Cobb Electric for materials in Larned, a town twenty-eight miles away. He went to several farms that had no electricity and talked to the farmers. They hired him to wire their farms and before long he had more work than he could handle. The word spread fast throughout the countryside, "Hire Howard; he's good, honest, and will do the job right." Being fired from the school district was the best thing that ever happened to him!

CHAPTER TWO

When Martha was three years old, she came down with pneumonia. Howard stayed home and was her nurse around the clock. The country doctor came to the house everyday to check on her. He came one night and could see she was slipping away. He gave Howard instructions on what to do and said, "I'll see you in the morning." Her fever broke during the night, and when the doctor came the next morning, he was amazed! He told Howard, "When I left here last night, I really didn't think she would make it through the night." Howard had not seen Elmer or Catherine since he took Martha from them in a rage several weeks after Merab died. When they heard how sick Martha was, they drove to town immediately. They walked in the front door with tears in their eyes and asked, "How is our girl?"

When the older children were in school, Howard still took Martha to work with him. She was his little helper. When he was in an attic, fishing the wire down through the wall to an outlet he made, Martha would reach up into the outlet with her little hand, grab the wire and pull it out of the hole. She knew how long he wanted it and would holler at him that she had it. Then she would clean up the mess with her own dustpan and broom. She also retrieved tools and materials for him from the car when he needed them. When Martha was five, he hired a young man to help him for the summer. When Howard sent him to the car for something and he couldn't find it, Martha would take him by the hand and point it out to him. She knew he didn't know what he was looking for and tried to fake it. Many times, it was right under his nose in plain sight. He was highly insulted to be getting help from this little snot-nosed kid. When it was time for Martha to start school the following year she said, "I can't go. Daddy needs my help on his jobs."

On the home front, the other three children fended for themselves. Delorse was a little slow mentally; due to a very high fever she had for several days when she was a baby. It was nothing short of a miracle that she lived through it. Laura was the one in charge and *charge she did*, just like the bull in the pasture that no one could manage but Laura, not even Howard. However, she was a very hard worker and managed most of the cooking, cleaning, washing and ironing, along with milking the cows, feeding the chickens and pigs, shoveling snow, washing the car, going to school, plus anything else that needed attention, without a lot of help from the others. Byron was very shy as a child, a real milk toast. He also had a serious deficiency; lack of ambition.

There was an outhouse in back. No water heater in the house; water had to be heated on the stove. They had mice, so the dishes and cookware had to be washed with hot soapy water before and after using them. No bathroom; they took baths in a tin tub in the middle of the kitchen floor. There was a pot-bellied stove in the dining room, plus a stove in the living room that burned oil. Neither one of them did very much for warmth during the severe winters in their two-story house that had the ventilation of a barn. The cold north winds blowing across the Kansas plains cut right through it. There was no garage for Howard's electrical equipment and materials. He stacked boxes of it against the walls in the living room, dining room, and the bedrooms downstairs. There were four bedrooms, but two of them were stuffed full up to the ceiling with Howard's junk. He never threw anything out. The three girls shared a bedroom upstairs with one double bed. In the hot summer months, Martha felt like she couldn't breath, sleeping between her sisters. There was no air conditioner, just fans. Dad and Byron shared a bedroom downstairs.

When the children cleaned house, they were never allowed to throw anything out—not even a newspaper. They had stacks of newspapers until the boy scouts had their paper drive. The scouts had to come back to pick them up later, after the children—with Dad's supervision—went through them, because important papers and checks from customers were always mixed in with them. There were also stacks of envelopes on the library table and piano in the living room. Dad knew what was in each one so the children couldn't move or mix them, just lift and dust. His car wasn't any better. The dashboard was loaded with stuff; including a lot of empty matchbooks with numbers written on the inside of the covers, part of Dad's accounting system. Only God and Dad knew what job the numbers were for and the meaning of them.

On Saturday, everyone but Dad took a bath. He would sneak over to the gym, in the schoolhouse one block away, with his towel and soap to take a shower. Then they all went to Larned to do errands and picked up materials Howard needed for his jobs. Many times, the children were left in the car for hours, even in the dead of the winter or the hottest part in the summer. Howard had no concept of time whatsoever! He usually arrived at a place at closing time, whether it was the bank, electrical supply store, grocery store, or clothing store. After he took care of business he would stand around and talk, completely oblivious to the fact that the employees wanted to go home and call it a day. People made allowances because they felt so sorry for him. Everywhere the family went, people always commented on how wonderful Howard was, raising four children all by himself. What a crock! He was king of the household and the children were his little white slaves!

CHAPTER THREE

When Martha was in the first grade, the teacher wrote on her report card to Dad, "Martha is not getting enough rest. She falls to sleep in class." Dad immediately started yelling when he read it, "The relatives have got to her teacher!" Martha was never tucked in or ever told when to go to bed; she just went on her own. Dad was never at fault! When Dad was hired to do a job, he gave the customers an estimate for time and materials. There were times when they added to the jobs, and Dad never told them how much more the additions would cost. Occasionally, the customer would not realize how much he added to the job, and would get irate when Dad gave him the bill. Every time this happened, Dad would yell and scream, "The relatives got to him and turned him against me!" The children would tease Dad, saying, "If the relatives did half of the things you blame on them, they wouldn't have the time to lead their own lives."

School was a real struggle for Delorse and they held her back two grades before she reached high school, putting her in the same grade as Laura. Byron had a small build and everyone considered him a sissy. His classmates picked on him constantly at school. One day in shop class, the teacher left for a while and the guys on the football team jerked off his pants and threw him outside in the sandbur patch. He ran home in his underwear, in tears. Dad had not left for work. After Byron explained what had happened and Dad picked the sandburs out of his butt, Dad stormed over to the school and went directly to the principal's office. The entire school could hear Howard yelling! Even Martha could hear him, downstairs in her classroom. She was amazed that Dad was going to bat for him, in view of the fact he was constantly yelling at Byron himself. Many times, he physically booted Byron out the door when it was way below freezing to get coal from the shed for the pot-bellied stove. Howard told the principal what happened and demanded, "What do you intend on doing about it?" The principal replied, "I don't know what I can do about it." Howard exploded, "You are a yellow bellied coward! You are afraid of them just because they are big bruisers! Get them in here now and I will handle it!" The boys were taken out of class and brought to the principal's office immediately. Howard proceeded to explain the facts of life to them, right in their faces. "If any one of you ever lays a hand on my boy again, I will come take care of you myself, and tear you from limb to limb. You will have to deal with someone your own size!" Every one of the boys left the office with their heads hanging low.

Eventually, Howard sold all the chickens, pigs, cows and the bull. However, they still planted a large garden every spring and did a lot of canning during the summer. When Laura turned sixteen, she was no longer Daddy's perfect little girl. Howard bought a panel truck for his business, so Laura had the car at home. She took the car without permission many times, so Howard started taking the car keys with him to work. She hot-wired the car and went out cruising anyway. Dad then removed the distributor cap before leaving for work. Laura discovered why the car wouldn't start, because she helped Dad work on the car and truck all the time, and just got another distributor cap from one of the old cars he still had in the backyard. Many times, Dad would be driving through Larned late at night, on the way home from a job, to find Laura cruising down the main drag with the car full of teenagers.

One night, Laura was out on a country road, drag racing with friends and rolled Dad's car two and half times. The car was totaled and her back was injured, leaving her with permanent damage. The County Sheriff asked Dad, "Did she have permission to drive the car that night?" Dad answered, "No, she didn't." The Sheriff replied, "I didn't hear that!" The Sheriff then asked, "She does have a driver's license, right?" Dad said, "No, she doesn't." The Sheriff replied again, "I didn't hear that!" He went on to explain, "If she didn't have a driver's license or have permission to drive the car that night, your car insurance wouldn't be worth a plug nickel!" He helped Dad make out the insurance claim and there was no problem. *Insurance fraud during the fifties, the good old days, in the Bible belt!*

The neighbors next door were in their late twenties and their marriage was on the rocks. Gene really had the hots for Laura and swept her off her feet. She thought he was her prince, there to rescue her from slavery. He was a truck driver and convinced her to run away with him. When Dad came home and discovered she was gone, he knew she was with Gene. He yelled at the rest of the kids to get in the car and drove thirty miles to Pratt. They stopped at a truck stop café to eat and he questioned a truck driver there who knew Gene. The man told Dad the name of the company in Wichita that Gene was working for. They drove on to Wichita and stayed with the Kesslers who had been friends of Dad's for twenty years. Dad went to the office of the trucking company and talked to the manager to find out when Gene would return from his long haul. The day he was expected, Dad sat in the car at the trucking company and waited for him. When he showed up, Dad was like a charging bull! He got out of the car and marched over to Gene and said, "If you don't tell me where you have my daughter, I'll have your ass in jail for kidnapping a minor!" Gene didn't argue with him and gave him the address. They found Laura in a big beautiful brick home, it was a mansion. She had answered an ad in the newspaper for a nanny, and was taking care of a little girl for room and board, plus a small salary. Laura was furious that Dad had found her, but never argued with him about going home. Gene's wife left town and they didn't see Gene or his wife again.

CHAPTER FOUR

Normally, Laura wouldn't be able to get Delorse to help with anything. Delorse could look busy doing absolutely nothing. Her lack of ambition was probably a good thing because she was usually a disaster waiting to happen. One day, Delorse had a rare moment of ambition and raked up the fall leaves in the front yard. She then lit a match to the pile of leaves, even though Dad preached to them many times. "Rake them, but never burn them." The fire started a trail immediately, burning right toward the house next door. There was no wall between the two properties to stop the fire. Delorse just stood there, screaming at the top of her lungs! Every man in town came to fight the fire and save the neighbor's house, while the rest of the townspeople came to watch. The town was very small and didn't have a fire department. The men were able to save the house only because it had a very high foundation of stone. After the fire was out and everyone had gone home, all four kids got busy and tried to cover the burned area with mulch, so Dad wouldn't find out about it. *What were they thinking? It was the news flash of half the county! The most excitement the town had seen in twenty years!*

One evening, Laura asked Delorse to keep an eye on the dinner she had cooking while she got ready for a date. Delorse was stirring a pot on the back burner, with the front burner on. She leaned over the stove with a spoon to get a taste, and the bottom of her blouse brushed over the front burner and caught on fire. She just stood there in the middle of the kitchen, screaming bloody murder, with the flames flying up in front of her face. Laura heard her and came running down the stairs.

She grabbed the back of the collar and yanked the blouse off of Delorse, sending the buttons flying, then ran outside with it and stomped out the fire. Fortunately, both of them only had minor burns.

A few months later, Dad was wiring a new house that was close to completion, right next door to Uncle Guy and Aunt Lula's house in Rozel. It was a small town, not much bigger than Trousdale. It was early evening and all the other workers had left for the day. Dad had started to pick up his tools when he heard someone driving around town honking the horn and hollering "Tornado coming! Tornado coming!" Dad finished packing up his tools, picked up his toolbox and headed for the back door. It wouldn't open, so he ran toward the front door. The next thing he knew, he was on the ground! There was a tree a few feet away and he crawled to it as fast as he could, fighting the very strong wind. He wrapped his arms around the trunk of the tree, locking his hands together and held on for dear life!

When it was over, he got up and looked around. The new house was completely gone, only the foundation was left! Next door, Uncle Guy and Aunt Lula's house was still there with only minor damage. The roof over their front porch had caved in from a large tree falling on it. When everyone came back to town after fleeing from the tornado, Uncle Guy and Aunt Lula were frantically looking for Dad. It was difficult driving in the streets, debris and large tree limbs were everywhere. They found Dad in the yard walking around in a daze. He was in shock. They tried to get him to stay for the night, but he said, "No, I've got to get home to the kids." He drove the forty-six miles to Trousdale very slowly. He was still dazed and in shock. When he walked into the house, all of the kids screamed, "Dad! What happened to you?" He answered, "Why do you ask?" They said, "You're covered with mud!" He was caked with mud from head to toe; all they could see of him were the whites of his eyes! When he started washing the mud off, his face and arms were full of cuts and scrapes.

The next day, they all went to Rozel to help Uncle Guy and Aunt Lula clean up. Before the tornado, they had a row of large trees; the only one left standing was the one Dad had hung on to for dear life! Everyone teased him that day, saying "The only reason that tree didn't go is because you held it down!"

CHAPTER FIVE

When Laura's boyfriend, who lived in Larned, couldn't afford the gas to come see her all the time, they introduced Delorse to his buddy Earl, so they could double date and share the gas expense. Within a few short weeks, after Delorse and Laura graduated from high school, Earl and Delorse wanted to get married, but Dad wanted both of the girls to go to college. Only God knows why he thought Delorse could make it in college; she had a tough time just getting through high school. Three weeks before they were leaving for college, Laura talked Delorse and Earl into eloping. She thought it would be fun and exciting! The night they were to elope, she found Delorse upstairs in bed instead of packing. Laura asked, "What are you doing? Earl's going to be here in one hour!" Delorse replied, "I've changed my mind. I'm not going." Laura said, "Oh, yes you are, and I'm going with you! I don't want to be around to face the music when Dad discovers you are gone!"

They drove all night so Dad couldn't find them. Earl and Delorse were married by a justice of the peace the next day. Earl didn't have much money so they got one motel room with two beds. Laura sat in the bathtub writing a letter to her boyfriend until they went to sleep. *How embarrassing for everyone—especially Delorse, who was as pure as the driven snow!*

When Dad came home very late that night, Byron didn't know a thing and Martha was spending the night with a friend. Dad went across town to pick up Martha at her friend's house, and woke up their entire household yelling, "Get in the car now! Your sisters have run off and we have to go find them!"

Dad always had a violent temper and yelled constantly when he was home, but this was nothing like Byron or Martha had ever seen—except once, when the cat ran into the house and landed on the breakfast table with all the food on it. Dad picked up the cat by the neck, threw her on the back porch and beat her to death with a broom. Then he screamed at Byron to go bury her. While Byron buried the cat, Laura and Delorse proceeded to cook breakfast over again, but no one could even think about eating. The children tried to act normal, but they were terrified!

Dad drove to Pratt and went to the police station, but they refused to do anything because both girls were over eighteen years old. Dad gave up and they went back home, but Byron and Martha walked on eggs around him for several weeks. They didn't even have the nerve to approach him about buying new school clothes. Both of them had outgrown almost all of their clothes, but they just quietly made do with what they had to start the new school year.

At ten years old, Martha became the lady of the house. She cooked, washed the dishes, and cleaned the house. Byron did the washing and ironing, but Martha ironed her own clothes. Dad would get home anytime from 6:00 p.m. to midnight, but she was supposed to be psychic and know when he would come home. He constantly yelled at her for never having supper ready. It never occurred to him that she should be in bed instead of cooking for him late at night when she had school the next day.

Several weeks later, Dad finally realized they needed new school clothes and took them to Larned to go shopping. They were in the Montgomery Ward store picking out a few things when a young saleslady walked up with a sheepish grin on her face and asked, "May I help you sir?" Dad looked up and there she was—his daughter Laura! After catching his breath, he started playing her silly little game and said, "Well, I don't know. Do you have some school clothes to fit these kids?"

After Dad bought the clothes, Laura gave him their address and invited them over for dinner. Earl, Delorse, and Laura rented an apartment together. Earl had a job in Great Bend with the Tribune Newspaper. Delorse stayed home and was already pregnant. Earl brazenly brought out their marriage certificate, saying, "See Dad, it's all legal! We are not living in sin!" Dad just looked at it with no comment and changed the subject.

CHAPTER SIX

The following year, Dad took Byron and Martha to California on vacation to visit relatives in August. Martha fell in love with California, and Dad's cousin Dorothy, who had no children of her own, fell in love with Martha. She asked Howard if he would leave Martha with her, to go to school there. Martha was elated! She adored Dorothy and her husband, Phil. Howard answered, "What would I do without my cook and bottle washer?" Martha just sat there, completely deflated. She thought, "Is that all I am, someone to cook and clean?" She made a promise to herself at that moment. Someday, she was going to move to California and kiss Kansas good-bye! During the past several years, she did a lot of daydreaming about the kind of life she wanted some day, but now she knew where she was going and shared that little secret with no one.

Two years later, Byron left home to go to college and Dad was down to one child. He became acutely aware of the fact that after Martha was gone, he would be alone. He did everything in his power to keep her from growing up, but Martha fought back hard. She was very independent and stubborn.

When Martha entered junior high, she thought long and hard on how she could change herself so the popular kids at school would like her. The first thing she did was tell everyone at school and her family that she wanted to be called Marty. She worked on coming out of her shell. In the process of making these changes, she learned that when she laughed at herself, everyone laughed with her instead of at her. Marty soon discovered she loved making people laugh, and became active in drama doing humorous readings.

Laura got married and had two boys in two years. Marty couldn't stand Laura's husband, Estel, because his mind never got out of the gutter. He got fresh with all the ladies by grabbing a boob or their butt. Marty tried to steer clear of him, but he would sneak up on her. Laura would either pretend she didn't see it or laugh it off. Marty hated him with every fiber of her body!

Howard's Mother was the sweetest and kindest lady God ever created, an angel in every way. One day when she was eighty years old, standing at the stove cooking, Estel walked up behind her and pinched her butt. Grandma picked up an empty black iron skillet and shoved it in his face so fast he didn't know what hit him! She then said to him, "If you ever come near me again, I'll flatten your face with this!"

One day Laura asked Marty, "Why don't you like Estel?" Marty told her, "Because he can't keep his damn hands to himself!" Laura's reply was, "Well, I don't like that either, but he doesn't mean anything by it. I trust him." Marty thought to herself, "Oh Lord! She is as sick as he is! They deserve each other!"

CHAPTER SEVEN

When the plumbing went bad and Dad never got around to repairing it, like everything else; they no longer had running water in the house. Marty had to pump all the water outside and haul it in. They had a five-gallon bucket under the kitchen sink to catch the used water, because the septic tank was no longer functional. Sometimes when Howard got home from work, the bucket under the sink would be almost overflowing and Marty would catch hell for not taking it out before it was so full. It never occurred to him that she was too little to be carrying that much weight.

On wash day, Marty pumped the water outside and carried it in a small bucket to the boiler on the stove, making many trips. Being so short, she had to stand on a chair to pour it into the big boiler on the stove to heat it. While the water was heating, she pumped and carried in water for the two tubs of rinse water, then carried the hot water bucket by bucket to the washing machine. She dipped the bucket into the boiler to fill it, and lowered it to the floor before getting off the chair. The biggest blessing of her life was when the washer broke down. Dad never got around to repairing it; he just took her to the Laundromat in Larned that had automatic washers and dryers. No more pumping water and hauling it in to do the laundry, putting everything through the wringer three times. The only water that had to be pumped now was for taking baths, cooking, washing dishes, and cleaning. No more hanging out the laundry on the clothesline. In the past, during winter, her hands were so chapped from hanging out wet clothes in the cold, they would bleed.

Usually, Dad and Marty went to Larned every Saturday. They did the errands and shopping. Then after she did the wash at the laundromat, they ate at a café and sometimes went to the movies. *Now there's an image every teenage girl dreams about, being seen with her father at the movies on a Saturday night!*

CHAPTER EIGHT

The Trousdale and Belpre schools were consolidated when Marty started her junior year in high school. Marty made many new friends, and was soon going steady with one of her new classmates, Larry. They had a lot of fun for several months until her best friend entered the picture. Larry dumped Marty for Dottie. More than her heart was broken, her pride took a beating, and she began to develop a real mistrust when it came to guys. Her father had no consideration for her and she saw a lot of unhappiness in Laura's life with Estel. Delorse's marriage to Earl certainly wasn't any love nest either. Marty didn't have another boyfriend the rest of her junior year, keeping a very tight hold on her heartstrings.

On a Saturday night, Jeanette, one of the girls at school, was having a party at her parent's café in Belpre. The café was closed for the party. Marty was invited and wanted to go so badly. After Dad and Marty did the shopping and laundry in Larned, she talked him into stopping at the party in Belpre. Dad insisted on going in with her to check out the situation. Jeanette's parents were not there, so Dad wouldn't let her stay. Some of the kids asked Marty, "Please stay," but the only thing she could do, is say, "I would love to but Dad won't let me." *This was 1959 in the middle of Kansas, the Bible belt. The kids in Kansas during that period of time never heard of drugs or smoking pot. They were really walking on the wild side if they got their hands on a six-pack of beer.*

Marty got the lead part in the junior class play. They had play practice every school night for six weeks. Juggling school, homework, play practice, and housework was certainly a challenge, and the house cleaning went by the wayside. She only did what had to be done: cooking, dishes, washing, and ironing. Dad made the comment several times, "I sure will be glad when this damn play is over with and this house starts looking like something again." Marty thought, "I could clean my heart out on this place and it would still look like shit with all of your crap! God forbid if you should ever lend a helping hand!"

After several weeks of being on her feet so much in play practice, Marty had such severe pains in her legs she would come home and go straight to bed, in tears. Dad talked about taking her to see Dr. Brenner; then a friend suggested that her back was the problem. So Dad took her to his chiropractor and he took x-rays. He looked at the x-rays and asked, "When was this child in a car accident, and just how bad was it?" Dad replied, "She has never been in a car accident." The chiropractor said, "That's impossible! I have never in all my years of practice seen a spine as bad as this on a young person!"

Marty had a problem of severe headaches during the past several years, but Dad never concerned himself about it. Her hips were twisted, causing the leg pain. She had severe scoliosis of the spine. The chiropractor decided that she must have had a mild case of polio when she was a small child. Marty said nothing and let it go, but she knew what caused it: the buckets of water she carried all the time and had been for several years. She went to the chiropractor on a regular basis after that, but still didn't receive any help from her Dad.

On the night of the play, two rows in the audience were filled with Marty's family; her Dad and brother; her sisters with their husbands and kids; her grandma with aunts and uncles. After the play, when people came up to Dad and told him, "Marty was great!" he popped his buttons. However, later that night, instead of telling her how proud he was of her, he let her know how embarrassed he was to have all the relatives come to the house after the play and see it a mess. He then said, "Now that we have this damn play over with, you can get back to your responsibilities!"

CHAPTER NINE

A few weeks later, Dad's temper finally caught up with him. He was going to mow the lawn and the power mower wouldn't start. After checking to make sure it had gas, he tried pulling the cord again. Then, in a fit of temper, he yanked on the cord again and again. All of a sudden, it started. His right foot had slipped underneath the mower while he was yanking on the cord, and the blades tore up his shoe and foot. He screamed at his friend Dave, who was a block away in the school garage. Dave heard him and came running. After rushing Dad to the hospital in Larned, Dave drove back to Belpre and got Marty out of school. He took her directly to the hospital. The doctor was not sure he could save Dad's foot. He lost two toes and the foot was really a mess.

Dave then took Marty back to Trousdale to pick up the car and some clothes so she could stay with Grandma in Larned. Her Grandmother lived alone and had for five years since Grandpa passed away. Marty drove back to Larned and stopped at Grandma's house. When she walked in, her brother was there. Grandma and Byron had a very grave look on their faces, like someone had died. Marty thought, "Oh my God, now what?" Before school let out that day, the gossip line had Dad's entire foot already amputated! Marty's closest friend was dating Byron at the time. Byron had called Gerry after she got home from school and she told him that his Dad had lost a foot! Byron lived in Great Bend, twenty-three miles from Larned, working at the Great Bend Tribune Newspaper. He flew in his car to Larned and stopped at Grandma's house first because he thought she would know what happened and be able to fill him in.

Late one night, the throbbing in Dad's foot woke him up. He rang for the nurse and she saw red streaks had started up his leg. The foot had beginning stages of blood poisoning. The nurse ran down the hall and returned to give him a shot with a very large needle. She then asked Dad what he wanted for dinner the next day. Dad replied, "Dinner! What about breakfast?" She informed him, "You are not going to be around for breakfast."

Marty stayed at Grandma's house and drove to Belpre everyday during the week to school. Three days after the accident, Marty had to go to Trousdale to get more clothes, pick up the mail, and some business papers to take care of for Dad. When she walked into the house, there was a strong burnt odor in the air. The stainless steel coffee pot had been plugged in for three days! Dad had left it plugged in when he went outside to mow the lawn. When Dave took Marty back to Trousdale to pick up the car and clothes, she had not noticed it. The coffee was completely gone and the interior of the pot was charred with burnt coffee. In addition to the pot being very hot, the cord and receptacle were also so hot; if Marty had not come home when she did, the house would have probably burned down!

Marty took care of business while Dad was in the hospital. She made collections and bank deposits, plus paid the bills. All Dad had to do was sign the checks she brought to him. She was worried sick about the possibility of Dad losing his foot. There was no way he could crawl in attics and underneath houses to wire with one foot. She didn't know what they would do if that happened, but she never let on to Dad.

When Dad was released from the hospital, Marty got him into the car with his crutches, and was immediately treated as though she didn't have a brain in her head. He yelled at her about anything and everything. Things were back to normal— no thanks, no appreciation, nothing!

Right after Dad was released from the hospital, Estel quit his job so he could help Dad with his business while his foot was healing. Laura and Estel moved their mobile home into the back yard. Dad said to Marty, "This is just great. I am laid up, and now I have four more mouths to feed, plus all of their debts that I will be making payments on too!"

Dad's foot had to be soaked in peroxide every day and redressed. When the dressing was removed, the odor of the foot was really gross. Laura couldn't handle it, so Marty did it for him. Still, Dad and Laura constantly ridiculed Marty, saying she was a self centered brat. Laura made snide remarks such as, "Marty thinks she's better than the rest of us. She's never home with her family." They didn't have a clue! Actually, she was hiding a lot of pain, hurt, anger, and loneliness inside, and was starved for acceptance. On the outside, she came across as being carefree. She only allowed people to see her as she wanted to be perceived.

CHAPTER TEN

In the fall of Marty's senior year, her closest friend, Gerry, was going with Dennis, who lived in Larned. Gerry and Dennis decided to play cupid and introduced Marty to Bob at a football game in Larned. His big brown eyes mesmerized Marty instantly! It was love at first sight! Marty's head was spinning for days. Dennis told Gerry that Bob was walking into walls. They became a foursome and double dated together.

Bob's mother, Mildred, started giving him a hard time about dating a girl from out of town. She didn't need the extra expense of gas. Mildred was divorced and raising Bob alone on a very tight budget. She had been in a car accident when Bob was a small child, and her right side was partially paralyzed. However, she still managed to work full time at the hospital in the medical records department.

Dad got a big wiring contract in the southern part of Kansas. It was too far to commute and the job was going to last for several months. They moved Laura and Estel's mobile home to Ashland to live in while doing the job. Marty stayed with Grandma and commuted to school in Belpre with one of her teachers who lived in Larned. This was indeed a very lucky break for Marty. She got away from Dad, Laura, and Laura's asshole husband, Estel. She could also see more of Bob, and she talked to him on the phone every day after school.

Marty loved Grandma dearly, but she was actually old enough to be Marty's great-grandmother. She was certainly not in touch with Marty's world of rock and roll. Marty met Bob's mother, Mildred, one day when she ran into them downtown. Bob called Marty later that day and asked if she would like to go to the basketball game in Kinsley with his mom. Bob was on the basketball team. Marty was ecstatic! She knew Bob had been fighting with his mom because of her. They really hit it off and Mildred became "Mom" to Marty in a very short period of time. The closer Mildred and Marty got, the further apart Bob and Marty became. He was a typical teenage boy, wanting to take off all the time with his buddies. Marty spent more time with Mom than with Bob. Mom was the first person in Marty's life who showed real interest in her, listening to her and caring about her problems. *Marty was starved for a mother's love and was thrilled to finally have a Mom!*

In the meantime, Bob and Marty played a little game of cat and mouse. Once in a while, he would go out with another girl; then Marty would go out with someone else just to get even with him. Near the end of the school year, he was quite interested in another girl in his own school, Sharon. Marty developed some sparks of her own for one of her classmates, Bill. Bob and Marty broke up when they graduated from high school, but Mildred remained to be her "Mom."

CHAPTER ELEVEN

Dad and Estel finished the job and they all moved back to Trousdale including Marty. Laura was pregnant with her third child and Dad was furious! Another mouth to feed! Estel got a job in Greensburg and they left. It was just Dad and Marty again. Marty counted the days until she could leave to go to Fort Hays State College. She couldn't wait to get away from Dad, be out of his control and no longer be his maid. The day finally came, but college turned out to be a very big disappointment. She was overwhelmed by it all, coming from a very small high school.

Laura had a beautiful baby girl, Diana, in October. At the same time Byron met the love of his life, Bernice, and they were married one year later, on Diana's first birthday. Bernice was very nice, but didn't make any effort to be close to Marty or anyone else, except Grandma.

During Marty's sophomore year of college, she saved every nickel she could out of the allowance she received from Dad, skimping on everything, even food. When she had saved enough, she packed up her clothes, called a taxi to take her to the depot and took a train to Denver, Colorado. The city lights were beautiful! There was excitement in the air on the busy city streets! She checked into a second rate hotel, bought a newspaper, and walked from one employment agency to another in high-heel shoes.

On the second day, she was in the process of taking a test at one agency when the lady interrupted her and asked Marty to come into her office and have a seat. She sat back in her chair and looked at Marty with her hands folded. Cautiously, she asked, "Marty, do you know a Howard Stilts?" Marty replied, "Yes, he is my father. Why do you ask?" The lady went on to explain, "Well, he just called and asked if you were here." Marty lost her cool and blurted out, "Oh my God, is he here?" The lady replied, "Yes, he is here in Denver, but I didn't tell him you were here now, only that I knew how to reach you. I asked him for the phone number of the place where he is staying, and told him I would give you the message. The reason I did that, I received a similar call one day and gave the man the information. He turned out to be the woman's ex-husband and went to the address I gave him with a gun and shot her. Since then, I refuse to give out information to anyone. Do you want to call your father?" After Marty said yes, she gave Marty the phone number and left the room to give her privacy. Marty dialed the number with her hands shaking like a leaf. Dad answered on the first ring. "Hi Daddy," she said, like a child caught with her hand in the cookie jar. Dad took a deep breath and asked, "Where are you?" She gave him the address and he was there in nothing flat. When he arrived, they gave each other a hug; then she saw the good-looking guy with him. Dad said, "This is Gib, Bill Baxter's friend, and he helped me find you."

Bill Baxter's mother had been Marty's landlady. Marty rented a room from Mrs. Baxter during her sophomore year of college in Hays, Kansas. When Mrs. Baxter discovered that Marty was gone, she called Howard and he drove up to Hays immediately. Then they found out Marty had bought a train ticket to Denver. Gib was going to college in Denver at the time, so they gave Dad his address and phone number so he could help Dad find her. They called Gib and explained the situation. Dad drove there that night. The next day, Gib spent hours on the phone calling employment agencies in the yellow pages to find her.

When Dad introduced Marty to Gib, he flashed her the most beautiful smile she had ever seen. Her only thought was, "Where has Bill been hiding a hunk like you? I've never seen you around the Baxter house." She thought she knew all of Bill's buddies. Bill was like a brother to her.

The first thing they did was check her out of the hotel and went to a coffee shop for dinner. This was the first real meal Marty had in some time. Then Gib suggested that they go to a little place in the mountains where the college kids loved to go for fun. It was a bar with a dance floor and it had the most fantastic view of the city lights. On weekends the bar had a live band, but tonight they played the jukebox. Gib asked Marty to dance several times. He was an excellent dancer with some smooth moves, and they really had a good time, in spite of the fact Dad was there. Dad was busy talking to other people and drinking beer.

The next day Dad and Marty left to go home, back to Trousdale, Kansas. *Dullsville!* Once they were in the car and headed out, Marty thought, "Oh boy, here it comes. This is going to be the lecture of my life." Dad began with, "Do you have any idea what you have put me through? What did you think you were doing? Do you know how much this little stunt of yours cost me?" Marty just let him go on and on, saying nothing. Finally, he looked at her, taking his eyes off the road for a second, "Well, what have you got to say for yourself?" Marty just looked at him, very calm, cool, and collected. Then she said, "I just met the guy I'm going to marry." Dad looked at her in astonishment! He started grinning and replied, "You know, I think you really mean that!"

After Dad and Marty arrived back home, they had a talk. *She managed to dodge the issue with him on the road because there would have been no escape for six hours.* Marty told her Dad, "I hate college and don't want to go back. I want to get a job. In high school and college, I have taken a lot of secretarial and accounting courses." Dad was livid! "I had four kids and don't have one college graduate! You are my last hope! If you don't go back to college, you are going to stay right here in Trousdale and rot! I'll work your ass off!" Marty stood her ground, saying, "What am I going to do with a college diploma? Teach school? No thank you! I want to work in an office; maybe be an executive secretary. Do you think by having a degree that

I'm going to work up to management? Get real! I am a woman! Maybe someday it will change, but right now, the men rule the world!"

The next day, Marty went over to a friend's house. When she came home, Dad was grinning from ear to ear. He proudly announced, "I'm taking you back to Hays tomorrow. You have a job interview with Southwestern Bell Telephone Company!" The next day, Marty had her interview with the Manager of the business office and the District Manager. She got the job! Marty became a Service Representative for Southwestern Bell Telephone Company in the business office. The timing of their call was unreal, like a miracle! The answer to Marty's prayers!

The manager of the business office, who was Marty's boss, told her several months later: After they had interviewed fifty women, he went down to the employment office to go through their files. He pulled out Marty's application and called for an interview. (One year prior to this, Marty had gone down to the employment office to fill out an application for a part-time job.)

CHAPTER TWELVE

G ib called Marty for a date when he came back to Hays to visit family and friends. Marty was crazy about him. Less than a month later, Gib transferred back to the college at Hays from Denver. The telephone company had sent Marty to a training class in Pratt, Kansas for six weeks. Gib and Marty wrote to each other constantly. When Marty returned to Hays after her training, they were an item.

Gib was completely disorganized, not dependable, nor thoughtful, or considerate. He never called for a date before the night they went out and he would still show up one hour late. Marty had fallen head over heels for a guy just like her father!

Marty loved her job and the people she worked with and made several new friends. A few months later, she bought a car from Gib's Dad, who owned the American Rambler dealership in Hays. Marty's new car was a 1962 Rambler convertible, metallic gold inside and out. Then she moved out of Mrs. Baxter's house into a large apartment with five other girls. The girls all had a ball going out at night in Marty's convertible when they didn't have dates.

Three weeks after buying the car, Marty went to Laura's for the weekend. Gib was in Denver for the summer, working on the railroad. Larry, Marty's boyfriend from high school, called before she left and asked if she had plans for the weekend. She said, "I'm going to my sister's, would you like to go with me?" Larry answered, "Sure, that will be great!" Marty drove to Belpre on the way and picked him up. As they were leaving, Larry's Mom said, "You kids drive careful! A lot of custom cutters are on the road now for harvest."

At harvest time in Kansas, there's a parade of combines, trucks and cars going through the countryside. They help the farmers harvest for a price. Once the wheat fields are ripe to cut, the farmers are always in a panic to get it cut as soon as possible. There's always that possibility the crops can be destroyed by hail, a tornado, or heavy rains.

Dad came down to Laura's too, for the celebration of Marty's birthday and Father's day. It was a fun and relaxing week-end. Dad and Laura didn't get on Marty's case with Larry there. Both of them thought the world of Larry, he really was a great guy.

Larry and Marty became good friends after she had time to get over him breaking up with her and having the "hots" for her best friend, Dottie. Larry and Dottie went together for a very short period of time and broke up. Marty came to realize, the whole thing was just crazy kid stuff.

Driving back to Belpre, Larry and Marty were going through Kinsley when a guy ran a stop sign and creamed the front end of Marty's car. He was a custom cutter from Oklahoma. Larry was driving, but there was no way he could have avoided the collision. The other guy hesitated at the stop sign and pulled out right in front of them. Larry's nose was broken and Marty had a fractured ankle, plus she wiped out the review mirror and then shattered the windshield with her forehead. (She scratched tiny slivers of glass out of her forehead for months and suffered with severe headaches.) The fractured ankle was no big deal, but she was broken hearted over her new car. Larry felt really bad about the car too. He said over and over, "Marty, your brand-new car! Your brand-new car!"

Marty tried to pacify Gib, telling him Larry, who was driving her car in the accident was a friend. He didn't buy it though, when he saw her car in his Dad's repair shop. (Gib's Dad had her wrecked car towed back to Hays.) The broken review mirror and the shattered windshield revealed that Marty was sitting in the middle of the seat next to Larry at the time of the accident. Gib was really pissed! She was sure that Gib wasn't keeping his pants zipped while working in Denver for the summer, but she didn't see Larry again.

Gib still lived at home with his parents and Marty was still in the apartment with five other girls. Marty decided to move into her own apartment so they could have some privacy. She had a ball fixing up her own little place. Now that she had her own apartment, Dad started coming up to Hays on weekends; so much for any privacy for Gib and Marty. (They didn't see each other during the week because of Gib's classes, homework, plus he worked part-time at his Dad's dealership.) Gib's parents and Howard got to be very close friends, and Gib's Mom introduced Howard to a friend of hers, Betty. Howard and Betty got to be a hot item in no time flat!

CHAPTER THIRTEEN

One Friday, Gib called Marty at the office to tell her he was going to take off for Denver and wasn't going to wait until she got off work to take her with him. He wanted to get out there early to sign up on the board to work a shift on the railroad. It didn't add up. Usually he called from Hays just before he left to sign up for a shift. She was suspicious.

During the school year, Gib went to Denver once a month, to work one shift to keep up his seniority on the railroad, for his job working full-time every summer. Usually, he would take her with him to Denver on these weekends.

Marty called a girlfriend of hers and asked, "How would you like to go to Denver with me for the week-end? I have friends there who have a pad where we can crash." Carol replied, "I'd love it! I've never been to Denver!" Carol and Marty threw some things together, filled the car with gas, and took off.

When they arrived in Denver five hours later, Marty drove straight to the apartment where Gib always stayed with friends. She knew they would be having a party—it was Friday night, TGIF! So Marty could arrive unexpectedly, Carol rang the security button to their apartment at the front door of the apartment complex. When one of the guys answered on the intercom, Carol said, as though they were old friends, "Hi, this is Carol!" He asked, "Carol who?" She answered, "You know me, this is Carol!" He pushed the button to unlock the door. Carol and Marty walked upstairs to the apartment, the door was partially open. Marty marched right in and saw exactly what she expected! There sat Gib, in an easy chair, with a girl on his lap in the corner of the room. They were very cozy, all wrapped up in each other! The girl, Bonnie, was supposed to be a friend of Marty's. Some friend!

One of the guys, Ray, said to Marty trying to lighten the moment, "Marty! How are you? How about a drink?" Marty replied, trying to sound light hearted, "We would love it! Ray, this is my friend Carol." Ray handed Marty and Carol their drinks. Marty's hands were shaking so badly she could hardly hold her glass. The entire room suddenly went deathly quiet. Everyone there knew Marty and was waiting for an explosion. When Gib looked up and saw Marty standing there, he stood up so fast that Bonnie almost fell on the floor! If Marty had not been so damn mad, she would have laughed. Gib grabbed Marty by the arm and pulled her into the hall. In a demanding tone he asked, "What are you doing here?" Marty laughed at him sadistically and answered, "The question is, my dear, what the hell are you doing?" He was embarrassed and frustrated, but most of all, he was mad at her because she caught him. He doggedly replied, "I've got a date." Marty retorted, "No kidding!" He said he would take Bonnie home and be back shortly. The party was breaking up and almost everyone had cleared out.

After Gib and Bonnie left, Marty said to Ray, "This is Carol's first time in Denver and I want to show her the town. I don't want to be here when he gets back. Let the bastard stew awhile. Why don't you go with us?" The three of them went all over, showing Carol the city lights and lovely neighborhoods; then stopped at a bar to have a drink. It was 4:30 a.m. by the time they made it back to Ray's apartment, but Gib still wasn't back from taking Bonnie home! By the time he did show up, Marty was so pissed she could have killed him with her bare hands! She asked, "Where in the hell have you been?" He said, "Bonnie's roommate had a date and he was drunk. She couldn't get rid of him, and I certainly couldn't leave until he did. I'm sorry but there was nothing I could do." Marty said, "The hell you say; you took the little bitch home and went to bed with her!" Marty stormed out the door with Carol right behind her.

The next day, Gib came over to see her. He turned on the charm and like a damn fool, Marty forgave him. He probably could have charmed the rattles right off of a rattlesnake. She never believed his story though, not for one second, and deep down she never trusted him again.

CHAPTER FOURTEEN

Marty received a settlement of five thousand dollars from the insurance company for her car accident. After the attorney took a third of it, she gave Dad fifteen hundred dollars to pay back what he spent on her college education.

One evening, Marty was sitting in a bar with her friend, June and June's husband, Smitty. Smitty said, "Marty, what are you doing wasting your life here in Hays, Kansas? As soon as I graduate from college, June and I are out of here! This is nowhere, man! You are single; nothing to tie you here." Marty started thinking about what Smitty had said, and thought, "Why am I hanging around here? I don't have any real commitment from Gib. The insurance money I have left from my car accident would cover my expenses until I got a job." She had always thought it would be great to be an airline stewardess and travel. This time, she informed Dad of her plans. She quit her job with the telephone company and moved to Denver. After several interviews with different airlines, she was called back for a second interview with Western Airlines. They were very interested in her. Marty was thrilled!

Then she received a call from Dad. He hurt his back while on the job and was laying in the hospital, in traction. Marty dropped everything and moved back to Kansas. Her Daddy needed her and she had to be there. Dad and Betty were getting married, and were going to live in Betty's house in Hays. Betty told Marty, "There's no need for you to rent a place; you are my daughter now, and you can stay right here with us."

It wasn't a month after Dad and Betty's wedding that Marty and Gib had a real battle one night on a date. Dad and Betty were out of town at the time. They came home to find Marty had packed up and left town. No one knew where she was, but Dad was sure she had gone back to Denver. Dad called Laura, but she had not heard from her. (Laura and her family lived in Boulder, about twenty miles from Denver.) Marty did go to Denver, but stayed with a friend for a couple of days until she found a nice apartment to share with two other girls. All of the renters in the entire apartment complex were young single adults. Every weekend was party time! She had an interview with Mountain Bell Telephone Company and was hired as a business order writer. Marty called Dad to tell him where she was, but made him promise not to tell Gib. But after her friends told her on the phone, that Gib was walking around like a little lost puppy, she called him. They made up, and went back and forth on weekends to see each other. After five months of him begging her to move back to Hays, she finally told him, "I'll move back when you decide to set a wedding date, but not until." Low and behold, much to her surprise, he decided they would get married that spring after his college graduation.

CHAPTER FIFTEEN

When Marty moved back to Hays, she stayed at Dad and Betty's house and enrolled in college again. She really buckled down and got straight A's just to prove to herself she could do it. Marty told her Dad, "I want to have a very small wedding. I can't afford a big church wedding and neither can you." Dad said, "No way—your sister Laura had a big church wedding and so are you. I'll come up with the money somehow." Marty started planning the wedding, going over all the costs with Dad for his approval. However, when the bills started coming in, Dad did not have the money to pay them. Gib had eight hundred dollars coming from selling cars at his Dad's dealership, but his mother informed him that they didn't owe him a damn cent. So Gib got a loan of five hundred dollars from a bank to cover the costs of the wedding and their honeymoon. Marty's Dad objected when the check was deposited into Gib's checking account saying, "It will look like Gib paid for the wedding." Marty let it go, but thought to herself, "Who in the hell does he think is going to make the payments?" Gib and Marty were screwed from both directions. Dad asked Marty what she wanted for a wedding gift, and she asked him for a place setting of her china. Dad told her to order it, but never got around to paying her.

Their wedding date was set a few days after Gib's graduation from college. He was joining the Navy to be a pilot like his older brother, Darrell. (Darrell had died in a Navy plane crash a few years before, off the coast of San Diego in California.) Gib's parents wanted no part of Gib following in Darrell's footsteps. They were happy when Gib went for his tests and was turned

down. He was slightly color blind and could not be a pilot. Gib
was devastated! This was his dream; all he ever wanted to be was
a pilot.

Gib had taken flying lessons for small aircraft and his Dad
owned a small plane. One day his Dad, Gib, Marty and another
friend were flying to Kansas City to pick up some new cars for the
dealership. It was windy that day and they shouldn't have been
flying at all. They made an emergency landing in Manhattan,
Kansas, where Gib's oldest brother lived. When his Dad made
the landing, he landed with the wind instead of against it. Any
pilot worth his salt would have known better, but his Dad was
a rotten pilot. When the plane touched the runway, one of the
front tires blew out. He lost control of the plane and it went all
over the runway. Marty prayed, like she had never prayed before
in her life! She was sure this was going to be curtains for all of
them! When the plane finally came to a stop, it was completely
off the runway in the open field next to the airport. The plane
was severely damaged, but only by the grace of God, no one was
hurt. The first thing out of his Dad's mouth was, "Don't tell your
mother about this!"

CHAPTER SIXTEEN

One Saturday night, Gib and Marty went out in Marty's car to the Varsity Bowl Drive-in, an eating place where the kids loved to hang out. Butch, a buddy of Gib's pulled up in his car alone. Without saying a word to Marty, Gib took the keys out of the ignition and went over to get in Butch's car. They sat there and talked for nearly an hour. Marty was burning. She would have just left, but he had the car keys, and her pride wouldn't let her go over to ask for them. Finally, when he did come back to the car, he didn't apologize; he didn't even act like there was anything to apologize for! Marty didn't say a word. When he pulled up to Dad and Betty's house, she got out of the car immediately and slammed the car door. As she walked into the house, she slammed that door too. After a few minutes, Gib came to the door. Marty refused to see him, so he handed her car keys to Betty and left in his own car. Dad and Betty wanted to know what happened and Marty told them. Dad failed to see why Marty was so upset. Why would he? He had left her in the car for hours, over and over again, when she was a child! The next day, Dad got worried and insisted that she should call Gib. Betty took Marty's side and said, "No way, he should call her. He owes her an apology." Marty was so furious that she didn't care if she ever saw him again. Gib finally called and turned on the charm up to ten on the Richter scale. Marty forgave him again like a damn fool.

The wedding plans went on, full speed ahead. Gib bought a new mobile home from his brother, who was a Mobile Home Dealer. They set it up in a mobile home park before the wedding. Marty cleaned it from top to bottom and moved everything into it. She lined all the cabinet shelves and put everything away. Everything had to be perfect for inspection when her sister Laura arrived from Colorado.

One week before the wedding, Marty blew up at Dad and Betty. Dad wasn't paying for the wedding and Betty had not helped Marty with any of the work, but they were still dictating to her about everything. Right from the beginning of the wedding plans, Marty wanted her friends for maid of honor and bridesmaids. No, the entire wedding party had to consist of family members. Then, all she heard from her entire family was constant bitching about the cost of their wedding clothes. In addition to all the work she was putting into the mobile home, Marty was taking her semester finals and finishing the last-minute tasks for the wedding. She packed a bag and went over to Sue's house to stay until the wedding. Sue was Marty's closest friend, and Marty needed to be in a place where she could breathe!

Gib thought Marty was kidding about the inspection, until Laura came in like an army drill sergeant! She marched around and yanked open every cabinet and closet door, expecting disorder. It was obvious that Laura was disappointed. Everything was neat, clean, and lined up perfectly. Her only comment was, "Hmmm, not bad."

Two days before the wedding, Gib and Marty got into it, big time! He took off with buddies of his to have fun while Marty was working her ass off. Marty lost it; she started crying and couldn't stop. She was exhausted. This was supposed to be the happiest time of her life, but she was miserable! Gib came over to Sue's after spending the evening with his buddies. They argued and talked for two hours in the car. Marty wasn't sure she was going through with the wedding. Finally, they called it a night. When Marty came into the house, Sue asked her, "How do you feel about him?" She replied, "Right now, I don't care if I ever lay eyes on him again." Sue gasped, "Marty! You are talking about the guy you are going to marry in less than thirty-six hours!" Marty replied, "I know, but that's how I feel! I would love to pack up my car and disappear, but I can't do it. All those people are on the road to come to my wedding as we speak. I would be leaving one hell of a mess!"

Gib came over the next day, full of remorse and was very sweet. She forgave him and like a damn fool decided to go ahead with the wedding.

Sue took Marty to the church to dress in the church basement where they had a bridal room. When it was time, Marty came up from the church basement in her lovely wedding gown. Sue was sitting at the guest book. She smiled at Marty and said, "You look beautiful." Dad and the rest of her family were not there. No surprise; they were always late for everything. Marty turned around and saw the church full of people waiting for the wedding to start, and went into a full-blown panic attack! It hit her like a bolt of lighting! She was looking for the nearest exit! Sue saw the look on Marty's face and knew exactly what she was thinking. She got up and walked over to Marty, took her by the shoulders and started shaking her. She said, "Marty! It's okay! You are going down that isle and everything will be just fine!" It was not just fine! The part of the ceremony when the bride and groom are kneeling; full of apprehension, Marty was praying, "Please God, help me make this marriage work."

The wedding reception was in the church basement. It wasn't elaborate by any means. Only mixed nuts, mints, and wedding cake were served with punch and coffee. Marty cut corners everywhere she could, especially on the flowers. The wedding cake was a gift from friends containing thirty-two dozen eggs. Marty only had to pay for the ingredients, just a portion of what it would have cost from a bakery. They had to deliver it to the church in separate layers and assembled it there. It was beautiful!

After the reception, Marty changed into her going-away dress and they were off on their honeymoon. They stopped at Abilene, Kansas. They had dinner and checked into a motel. The first thing Gib did was call his Mother! Even his Mother was shocked to receive a call from him on his Wedding Night! Marty undressed in the bathroom and put on her beautiful lingerie gown. She came out to make her grand entrance, and

Gib was playing with his two-way radio he brought with him. He didn't even bother to look up. There was no point for him to be interested. Marty had already told him that her period started that day. She had not given it a thought when deciding on the wedding date.

The date was set so they could leave for Florida right after the wedding, just a few days after Gib's college graduation. They were moving to Florida for Gib's training in the Navy. All of those plans went up in smoke when he found out he was colorblind and could not be a pilot.

The next day, they drove to Kansas City and checked into a hotel. After dinner, they went to a nightclub. Gib didn't even ask her to dance. Their final destination was the *Lake of the Ozarks* in Missouri. They drove around to enjoy the beautiful countryside. Marty was with the man she had just promised to love for the rest of her life and was bored out of her skull!

CHAPTER SEVENTEEN

The minute they returned home from their honeymoon, Gib had to go to the garage to see his parents. He went from part-time to full-time at his Dad's dealership. The salary he received was next to starvation wages and his hours were long. He was manager of the parts department and was on call twenty-four hours a day, seven days a week for their wrecker service.

Marty was selling her car to get rid of the car payment. Her Dad wouldn't hear of it. He said he wanted the car and would take over the payments. The car title and loan were in both of their names, but when Dad was late with a payment, the bank called Marty. She finally told him, "You are ruining my credit! I'm selling the car!" Dad said "No, I want that car!" Marty told him, "If I get one more call from the bank, I'm selling it!" The bank didn't call Marty again.

It was very seldom that Gib and Marty had a chance to socialize with their friends. They were with their parents the majority of the time. Marty was never consulted about their plans with Gib's parents, she was lucky to be informed. When they did get a chance to go bowling with friends, his parents would show up at the bowling alley to join them. Marty thought she had married into a mafia family. Everything was for the *family*.

Gib went with his Dad, Ray, to Kansas City for a dealer convention. Marty wanted to go, but Ray told her that wives were not allowed. A few days after Ray and Gib returned; a letter came in the mail about the convention addressed to Mr. and Mrs. Gib Kobler. They made a statement in the letter on how pleased they were that so many of the wives were there.

Marty had already heard rumors about her father-in-law screwing around with different *ladies* in town. A few weeks later, Marty had a severe kidney infection and had to be hospitalized. She became friends with her roommate and they talked about the problems in their lives. Dad and Betty came to see Marty in the hospital, as well as her mother-in-law, Charlotte. After they left, Marty's roommate asked a few questions about her family and in-laws, and wanted to know their last names. When Marty told her, the roommate said, "Oh my God!" When Marty asked what was wrong she replied, "I really hate to tell you this, but your father married a whore! She has been screwing around for years and right now your step-mother is screwing around with your father-in-law!" Marty didn't know whether to laugh or scream, but she knew that she had to keep this explosive information to herself.

Gib and Marty's marriage was falling apart at the seams. It certainly started out on very shaky ground, but things were getting even worse. They were always fighting and Gib loved slapping her around—after all he was king shit! His family was big in the community, and Marty was someone to wipe his feet on. One night they got into it and he backhanded her one; his ring struck her cheek bone and it started bleeding. She ran out the door and walked for six blocks to Dad and Betty's house in the rain. Soaked to the skin, she walked into their house, unaware that Gib's parents were there. She tried to leave, but it was too late; all four of them wanted to know what happened. For once in her life, Marty's Dad was in her corner and said, "You are spending the night here."

Charlotte, Marty's mother-in-law, talked to her later. Marty asked, "Where did Gib get the idea that it's okay to hit a woman? Did he ever see his Dad slap you?" Her reply was, "Only when I deserved it. Let me tell you something about guys Marty, and the sooner you accept this, the better off you'll be. There's only two things guys care about in this world, having their stomachs full and their balls empty."

CHAPTER EIGHTEEN

Marty was struggling with her household budget. She had not been able to find a job. Jobs were hard to come by in Hays, with many wives working to put their husbands through college. She never spent a dime on clothes for herself, but if Gib needed anything his Dad took him to a store and bought it for him.

Then Gib decided he wanted a new car. Marty screamed and said, "We can't afford a new car! We can't afford the payments! Our old cars are just fine and their paid for!" Gib's Dad informed Marty, "If Gib wants a new car, he will have a new car, and anything that goes on down here at the garage is none of your damn business!" So Gib got his new car. In order to do this, Gib had the car financed with one bank. Then he went down to another bank and took out a six-month note to cover the car payments. He was going to keep the car for six months, then sell it. Since he bought the car at his Dad's cost, he thought he was going to make money on it, and then do the same thing over again.

Sue, Marty's dearest friend, moved to Southern California with her husband, Leo and their children. When they left, Marty told her, "I hate to see you go, but I'm coming out to join you eventually. Life really stinks here." Sue said, "I sure hope you can, we're leaving all of our family and friends."

Shortly after Sue and Leo left, Marty finally found a job as the head cashier at the American Finance Company. By then, she was really fed up, big time! When she received her first pay check, she went down to a bank and opened a savings account in her name only. Marty told Gib, "I'm saving all of my paychecks.

It's my California or bust fund. As soon as I have saved enough money, I'm out of here! Whether you come or not, is entirely up to you, but I'm going with or without you!"

A few months later, Gib had a car payment due and no money to pay it, his six-month note was due at another bank, and he had not sold his car. He begged Marty to draw out money from her savings account to save his ass. Marty just looked at him with a smile on her face and said, "You know, it will be a cold day in Hell when money that I earned myself pays for something that was none of my damn business! You go tell your daddy that, and also tell him to stick it right up his ass! I don't give a damn!" His dad got the car sold and didn't say one word to Marty.

After it was apparent to Gib's parents that Marty was serious about leaving and Gib decided he was going with her, Marty knew they would have loved putting a hit out on her. Gib came home one day from work and said, "Dad wants to know if he paid me five hundred dollars a month, would you forget about moving to California?" (This would have almost doubled Gib's salary.) Marty smiled at him and replied, "You tell your father that I wouldn't stay if he paid you five thousand dollars a month!"

Marty's Dad tried to talk her out of quitting her job. He said, "What if you get out there and don't find a job? If you do, you could come back here and then give them their two week notice." Marty replied, "First of all, anyone in California needing someone for a position needs her now, not a month from now. Second of all, I'm not going out there to look for a job, I'm going out there to find one!"

After Marty turned in her letter of resignation to her manager, Steve, he called the district manager to tell him that Marty was quitting and moving to California with her husband. The district manager said, "Talk her out of it! Give her a raise! Don't let her go; she is the best you've ever had in that office!" Steve told her what the district manager had said and then added, "I hate like hell to see you go, but I'm not going to even try to talk you out of it. This is the last of the great no places! You go to California and I wish you nothing but the very best!"

Steve gave her a beautiful letter of recommendation to take with her. He made it sound like she walked on water.

Two weeks later, Gib and Marty left for California to start a new life.

CHAPTER NINETEEN

Gib and Marty drove straight through to Southern California, stopping only for gas and to eat. They arrived at Sue and Leo's house at six-thirty the next morning. Marty had written to Sue about their plans. Sue was so excited, she wrote back and said, "You will stay with us as long as you want, we are counting the days!"

California was beautiful! Palm trees and lush landscaping everywhere! It was in the fall of 1965, in the days when Southern California was still the land of milk and honey. Marty and Gib started working with employment agencies the next day.

Sue and Leo both worked and had two children, so their weekends were very busy doing the wash, yard work, and cleaning house. They said to Gib and Marty the first weekend after they arrived, "You go have fun. You won't have a lot of time for fun after you find jobs and get settled." So Gib and Marty took off for the beach. On the way, they saw some kids in a car with a Kansas tag. They talked back and forth at stoplights. Gib asked them, "Do you live here?" They yelled back, "Yes and we love it! This is paradise, man!"

Gib and Marty had a ball at the beach. It had been twelve years since Marty saw the Pacific Ocean; when she came to California on vacation with her dad and brother in 1953. She made a promise to herself then, at the ripe old age of eleven, that she would live there someday. Spinning around with her arms spread out like an eagle, feeling the ocean breeze in her face, she announced, "I'm here! I've made it!"

They planned to have their mobile home moved to California. It was going to be costly, but they loved their house.

After driving all over the area, they found a lovely mobile home park for *adults only* very close to Arcadia; a beautiful town. The manager of the park didn't give them the time of day at first, telling them he had no vacancies. They were very young, and most of the residents were retired or close to it. Marty talked to him, telling him all about themselves. Gib explained, "Our mobile home is just sixteen months old and it was from a mobile home show. It's loaded with extras and upgrades. We have no pets and no children." The manager said, "I have one space that's going to be vacant at the end of the month." They gave him a deposit and filled out the papers. They were going to be right next to the swimming pool, landscaped beautifully with palm trees. Every space had a patio, driveway, and a small yard.

Gib went back to Kansas on a train for two weeks, to pick up their second car and to hire a company to move their mobile home to California. Marty's Dad helped him get the house ready, putting on the wheels and removing the blocks. Marty had already packed everything inside so it would be secure in shipment. Gib's Dad took him shopping and bought him a new suit for job interviews. He also co-signed a loan for the cost of moving the mobile home. He told Gib, "Don't tell your mother I did all this, it's our little secret." When Gib went to pick up his final check from his mom, she said, "You didn't do me a damn bit of good around here the last couple of weeks, always taking off to take care of that damn trailer! I don't owe you a thing!"

A few days after Gib returned to California, he found a job with Mobil Oil Company, in their accounting department in downtown L.A. Marty was hired by Euclid, a division of General Motors, located in the City of Industry. She was in the accounting department too. Both of them had more than doubled their salaries, plus receiving fantastic benefits. The mobile home arrived with no problems and no damage. They loved California and their new jobs.

Marty made up her new budget. They had a lot of debt hanging over them. They had ninety days to have their skirting installed around the bottom of the house, plus a porch and awning for the patio. The park had strict rules on what they would accept. Marty opened a savings account in her name only. She figured how much she could save each month after the payments and expenses, allowing only twenty dollars a month for entertainment. Then she made a timetable for when she would have enough to pay off each debt. She started on the small debts first and worked her way up. Gib bitched and complained, "Why can't we do something this weekend?" Marty would reply, "Because we have already spent twenty dollars on entertainment this month." He would argue, "But you have all that money in the bank!" She would reply, "You just forget that money is there. We are in debt up to our eyeballs and I'm going to get us out!" They went to the beach a lot on Sundays with friends. Marty worked a lot of overtime and earned more money than Gib, which made it tough on his precious male ego.

Gib joined a car pool, to alleviate the problem and expense of parking in downtown L.A. He came home one night and said he lost the car pool and started driving alone everyday. Then he enrolled in a night class. One night when he was in class, Marty answered the phone and a gal asked in a very sexy voice, "Hello. Is Gibby there?" Marty replied, "No, may I take a message?" She said, "Please tell Gibby I won't be riding with him in the morning." Marty replied, "I will tell him!" When Gib got home, Marty casually asked him, "Have you had any luck finding another car pool?" The answer was no. Marty replied, "Well, your little girlfriend called and said she won't be riding with you tomorrow." He turned sixteen colors of the rainbow! They got into a knock-down drag out!

It was amazing how fast he was able to find another car pool.

CHAPTER TWENTY

It was in the spring, Marty received a call one night from Gib, after she got home from work. He said, "I have to work late, pick me up at nine." Marty replied, "Fine, I'll see you then." Marty pulled up in front and waited in a fifteen minute parking zone. He came out of the building with another guy and they got in the car. Gib explained, "This is Frank, who works with me in the same office and we are in the same car pool, so he needs a ride home too." Frank didn't live far from them and they chatted all the way home. He was recently divorced. Marty thought Frank was the most egotistical guy she had ever met and did not like him. However, Gib and Frank became buddies so Marty had him over occasionally for dinner and they played cards.

After Marty got to know Frank, she thought he was a nice guy and decided to fix him up with Pam, a close friend of hers and colleague. She invited Pam for dinner after work and Gib invited Frank over the same night. After dinner, they tried teaching Pam how to play pinochle. It was a little frustrating when she kept referring to "clubs" as puppy dog feet and "spades" as little shovels. After Pam left, Frank said, "She is a nice girl, but not my cup of tea. I think she is a little queen bee." Pam was a very pretty girl, great body, intelligent, and dressed beautifully; but Frank really nailed her right on the head. The next day at work, Pam asked Marty, "Did you give Frank my phone number?" Marty sidestepped the question because she didn't want to hurt Pam's feelings. She asked about Frank several times, but Marty kept dodging the issue.

When Frank came over for dinner, Gib was constantly criticizing Marty to Frank. He said, "She's so stupid that she pays a bill as soon as she receives it." Frank answered, "Don't look at me, I'm the same way." Gib complained about her stupid budget and master plan to pay everything off because she hated debts. Frank replied, "Don't look at me, I feel the same way. I'm a cash man. If I don't have the money, I don't buy it." Gib kept complaining and criticizing Marty constantly about everything and anything. He complained that she was such a neat nut and constantly cleaned. Frank just kept on saying, "Don't look at me, I'm the same way." After this happened many times, Marty said to Gib in Frank's presence, "Why can't you be more like Frank? I'm going to divorce you and marry Frank!" *She really thought she was kidding.*

Marty told Gib several times, "You need to take my car in; the brakes are going on it." As usual, he never got around to it. She was driving to work one day and a child darted out in front of her. The brakes failed when she slammed them into the floorboard. She swerved the car as much as possible, missing the child by a hair. The child was fine. He was in better shape than Marty, who was shaking like a leaf.

When she walked into the office, her supervisor said to her, "You're late!" with a smile on his face. Marty burst into tears. The manager, Mr. Lowe, called her into his office and asked, "Marty, what's wrong? What's going on with you?" She told him what happened on her way to work. He said, "I understand completely how that would upset you, but you have not been yourself lately. What's wrong?" She just blurted out, "I think I'm pregnant!" He exclaimed, "But that's good news!" Marty really got upset then and said, "No it's not! We can't afford a baby now! I don't need a child anyway, I've already got one; my husband!" Mr. Lowe tried to calm her down and said, "Marty, most guys don't grow up until they become a father themselves." He decided she needed the day off and had Cal, her supervisor, drive her home because of the problem with the brakes. The car went into the shop immediately. A couple of days later, Marty started her period, and she thanked God from the bottom of her heart she wasn't pregnant! Mr. Lowe gave her a big smile when she told him *false alarm.*

There were three accounting girls: Linda, Pam, and Marty. When Linda got married and quit her job, Mr. Lowe called Pam and Marty into his office. He said, "I have bad news for you both. We are not going to replace Linda because of the recession we are in now. It will be up to the two of you to do her job, in addition to your own." Pam and Marty both reassured Mr. Lowe they could handle it, even though that meant more over-time. Marty told him, "Actually, I am relieved. I've been worried about being laid off because of the recession, since I'm at the bottom of seniority in the accounting department." Mr. Lowe replied, "Oh, I really wish you had come to me with your concern so I could have put your mind to rest. If it came to that, I would have fired Linda before I laid you off. Linda's work hasn't been good for some time."

One day, out of the blue, the GM auditors walked in the door. Auditors were easy to spot when they walked into an office; they had a certain air and attitude about them. Then Marty would think to herself, "Oh great! As if I don't have enough to do; now I get to be interrupted constantly with their questions and requests for different records." After the auditors completed their audit and left, Mr. Lowe called Pam and Marty into his office. He said, "I really shouldn't tell you girls this but it's too good to keep. In my final meeting with the auditors, they told me I have two of the best accounting clerks in General Motors! Both of you can be very proud of that, because the GM auditors are as tough as they come in the corporate world! They just don't go around and hand out compliments like that to anyone!" Marty received a very nice raise later and Gib belittled it. He did everything he could to destroy her self-esteem, just like her dad and her sister Laura had done her entire life.

Gib's little brother, Arden, came out to California for the summer. He got a job and lived with them, so Marty had two guys to wait on hand and foot. There were a lot of problems and their marriage was on the rocks. Gib's nose was glued to the TV when he was home and their sex life had become nonexistent even before Arden arrived on the scene. Marty thought a weekend away would help, and drew money out of savings. They went to San Francisco on the Fourth of July weekend and left Arden on his own with his buddies. The whole trip was a total disaster, just like their honeymoon. Marty was bored out of her mind! On the way home, they spent the night in Santa Barbara and went to a lovely place with live music and dancing. After dinner, Gib asked Marty to dance. They were slow-dancing when out of the blue; he asked her, "Marty, do you still love me?" She answered, "No." Marty was surprised as much as he was by her answer. It just came out! Then she started thinking about it and realized it was true! She not only no longer loved him, but also had lost total respect for him. There was nothing there. She didn't even know what she ever saw in him. He had slowly killed all the love she ever had for him with all of his lies, not being dependable or trustworthy. It was over.

Two weeks after Arden returned to Kansas to start college, Marty went over to see Frank without Gib. She needed to talk to a friend who had been divorced, and Frank was the only one she knew. Marty wasn't sure what kind of an attitude she would receive from Frank. She had visions of him saying, "You women are all alike! You are going to walk out on Gib just like Carol walked out on me!" She decided to bite the bullet and take her chances. Marty took a deep breath and knocked on his door. Frank was surprised to see her. He told her to come in and offered her a drink. She took the drink and then said, "I need to talk. I've really had it with Gib." Frank asked, "What do you want to do?" Marty answered, "I want to move out and get a divorce. I can't take it anymore." He just looked at her and thought a minute, then he asked, "Are you sure that's what you want?" Marty said, "Yes, I am." He asked again, "Are you *really* sure that's what you want?" She repeated herself again with more conviction, "Yes, I am!" Then he said, "I don't want to open my mouth if you are not sure that's what you want." Marty reassured him again, so Frank began, "I don't know how you took it as long as you did. He treats you like a piece of shit!" Marty was flabbergasted! She couldn't believe the support she was getting from Frank. She said, "It's going to be difficult to get out of there. He is dead set against getting a divorce because there has never been a divorce in the history of his family. He says there is no way in hell that he is going to be the first! There's never been one in mine either, but if I stay with him, I'm going to end up in a straight jacket!" Frank asked, "Do you want some help? We could move you out while he's at his night class." She replied, "That would be great!"

It had been one year since Gib and Marty moved to California. She had worked really hard paying off their debts, and the only one left was on the mobile home. Gib could make it now without her paycheck. She found a small furnished apartment that she could afford in Arcadia. Frank picked up a lot of empty boxes at the grocery store and came over one night after Gib left for class. Frank and Marty worked fast, packing up most of the kitchen, the decorative accessories, her bathroom items, clothes, and some of the linens. They moved like lighting! Two hours later, they had both of their cars packed full and were out of there before Gib got home.

It was two days before Marty got the nerve to call her Dad in Kansas. As soon as Dad heard her voice, he let her have it with both barrels. "Gib called me the night you moved out, as soon as he discovered you were gone. You have broken his heart. What do you think you are doing? Have you lost your mind? He will get drafted now without his married status and they'll send him to Vietnam. He's going to get killed! How are you going to live with that on your conscious?" Marty tried to tell her Dad, "You don't know what I've been going through, he treats me like shit! I can't take it anymore!" She got the standard answer that she had been getting her entire life, whenever she was stupid enough to go to him with her problems, "You don't know what problems are, just wait until you hear mine!" Then he would proceed to unload on her.

Gib called Marty at her office and she agreed to see him to discuss the divorce. He said, "Why now? We've got it made! Everything is paid off except the mobile home." She replied, "This has nothing to do with money. It has to do with our marriage, it stinks!" Gib blasted her, "The only reason I agreed to move to California is to try to save this marriage! You took me away from all my family and friends!" Marty replied, "I failed to realize something. I could move you to China, but that's not going to change you."

Marty filed for divorce. Her attorney thought she was crazy because she didn't want a settlement. He said she could keep the mobile home and make him pay for it with the grounds she had for the divorce. Other than household items, accessories, and her personal things, she took nothing but a stereo she bought, a coffee table and end table. She had movers pick up the stereo and two tables the day after she moved out, while Gib was at work. She didn't want anything; but out of the marriage. The divorce attorney gave her a smile and said, "You are certainly a different breed than my other clients. I'm used to women coming in here wanting to leave their husband nothing but the shirt on his back. Sometimes I think they want that too!"

Frank and Marty saw a lot of each other, as friends. She would go over to his apartment and they watched TV. Marty didn't have a TV; she left it with Gib. She invited Frank over for dinner one night. Gib found out where she was living and came over that same night. He walked in and saw the table set for two with her china and silver. He asked in a demanding tone, "Who's coming for dinner?" Marty retorted, "It's none of your damn business!" Gib stood there a minute looking at her, and then suddenly it hit him. "It's Frank, isn't it?" Marty said, "Yes it is, so what." He started screaming at her, "Frank was my buddy; how could you do this?" He went on and on. Marty looked at the clock and realized that Frank was late. He was never late for anything—the exact opposite of Gib. Then it hit her and she thought, "Frank saw Gib's car parked out front; he's going around the block twenty times waiting for Gib to leave." Gib didn't leave, and refused to until Frank got there. He wanted to talk to Frank. Finally, Marty walked out to the street in front of the apartment complex. In a couple of minutes, she saw Frank coming down the street and she motioned for him to pull over. She told him, "Gib refuses to leave until he talks to you." Frank parked the car and Gib was right there yelling at him, "How could you do this? You were my friend!" The three of them were standing in the street with cars rushing by. Marty said to both of them, "Let's not stand out here in the middle of traffic, go inside." As they entered her apartment, Gib immediately started yelling again. Marty ran around closing all the windows. She thought, "Oh Lord, I'm going to get evicted!" Frank sat down on the sofa; calm, cool, and collected. He let Gib rave on and on about how he was a friend; asking over and over how could he do this to a friend? After Gib started winding down, Frank asked, "Are you finished? May I speak now?" Gib answered, "Yes! What have you got to say for yourself?" Frank took a deep breath and started in, "First of all, let me state a few facts. Marty is a very cute girl and she is a lot of fun to be with. She is a damn good housekeeper and cook. She's intelligent, responsible, and has a great job too." Raising his voice, Frank added, "You treated her like a piece of shit! You don't know what you had there! You blew it and you have no one to blame but yourself!" Gib didn't even try to rebuttal; he just started in again with, "But you were my friend!" Frank answered, "Well Gib, let me ask you this: What would be more important to you; a friendship with a buddy, or a possible future with a great lifetime partner?" Marty nearly fainted! She had no idea of the feelings Frank had for her! He had just been her friend. Gib took off in a huff at that point. After he left, Marty finished preparing dinner and they sat down to eat; laughing and talking about what an ass Gib was, big time. Frank helped her clean up after dinner and then they sat down to have a talk. Marty told him, "I had no idea of how you felt about me." Frank replied, "You never would have either if you had not left him. I would never get involved with a married woman, much less a wife of a friend!" He kissed her good night and left. Marty undressed and crawled in bed. She laid there thinking about everything that had happened during the course of the evening and thought, "I think I've finally found a wonderful guy who really cares. I have found my Prince!"

CHAPTER TWENTY-ONE

One day at the office, Pam suggested to Marty, "Why don't we go to a bar some night. It's really fun." Marty replied, "Bars are not my scene, Pam. Actually, I've been seeing a lot of Frank." Pam sat there in shock, just looking at her for a minute. Then suddenly exclaimed, "So that's why you wouldn't give Frank my phone number. You wanted him for yourself!" Marty just smiled and said nothing. It would have crushed Pam's ego, if she knew Frank wasn't interested in her, but was now interested in Marty. After all, Pam was queen bee of the office.

Frank grew up in Arcadia, California and his entire family lived in the vicinity. He took Marty over to meet his sister, her husband, and two little girls one evening. Marge and Dick seemed very nice and their daughters, Melody and Terri were adorable.

A couple of weeks before Christmas, the family decided to have a tree trimming party at Frank's apartment. Marty really hit it off with Frank's Mom. It was instant bonding. She was the greatest and treated Marty like she was already a member of the family. Mom, Marge, and Marty were the Christmas tree trimmers. The three of them talked and laughed like they had known each other for years. Then there was Frank's Dad. He sat back on the end of the sofa all night, with his arms folded across his chest, looking just like a mad bull dog, not saying two words to anyone all night!

Long before she had moved out and filed for divorce, Marty bought train tickets for herself and Gib to go back to Kansas for Christmas. Frank took Marty to the train station and there was Gib, still going on the same train! Marty thought, "Oh boy, this is going to be a riot. We'll be on this damn train together for twenty-six hours." She went to the club car a lot and made friends on the train. It really worked out well because with other people around, Gib couldn't give her a hard time. When the train pulled into Dodge City, Kansas where her Dad was meeting her, Gib's Dad was there too picking up Gib.

Marty had her heavy winter coat ready to put on when the train pulled into Dodge, so she was aware that it was going to be cold. It was December and they were in the middle of Kansas. However, when she stepped off the train, her reaction was, "Holy cow!" It was cold all right, but the typical cold north winds that blew through the Kansas plains in the winter cut right through her. The wind almost knocked her right off her feet! After living in the beautiful climate of Southern California for only fifteen months, she had already forgotten how that cold wind felt! Dad was excited to see her and welcomed her with open arms. After having dinner at a coffee shop, they drove on to Hays.

Dad and Betty had the whole family there for Christmas. You couldn't hear yourself think with everyone talking at once. Everyone took their turn, preaching to Marty about the divorce. Marty thought a hundred times, "Why on earth did I think I was homesick?" The day before Christmas, Marty went to get her hair done. When she returned, Gib and his family were there! The second she walked in the door, Dad grabbed her by the arm and yanked her into the hall, away from everyone else. Marty was pissed and asked her Dad, "What the hell are they doing here?" Dad answered in a belligerent tone, "Never mind that; they are family, whether you like it or not! What I want to know, who in the hell is Frank?" Marty asked in a tone of excitement, "Oh, did he call?" Dad replied, "No, this came while you were out," waving a telegram in her face. Marty grabbed the telegram to read it. Dad explained that he had opened it because he thought it was bad news. It said, "Sweetheart, wishing you all the joys and happiness of the holiday season. Merry Christmas. Love Always, Frank." Dad was furious and demanded, "Answer my question! Who in the hell is Frank?" Marty said, "He's a really nice guy I've been dating." Dad asked if he had ever been married. Marty answered yes. Then he asked, "Is he divorced?" Again, Marty answered yes. Dad exploded, "You are dating a divorced man?" Marty replied, "So what, I'm a divorced woman, or in the process of being divorced." Dad retorted, "That's different!" Marty walked off and went to the kitchen to help Betty with dinner, ignoring Gib and his family. She smiled and thought, "Thank God Dad didn't see Frank's letter that came yesterday; he would have had a stroke!" Frank wrote, "I MISS YOU!" in huge caps. He also wrote, "I wish you were here so we could spend Christmas together, you with your red bow and me with my green bow. I'm counting the hours until you will be back here. I am counting the hours because I can't count high enough for the minutes or seconds. Write soon if you are not frozen. If so, I'll defrost you! Seriously though, I do miss you and wish you were here. I have a notion that I Love You, Frank"

Marty was on the train back to California the next day, and not a minute too soon. Gib didn't bug her on the trip back; he was feeling defeated since Marty didn't have the time of day for him while they were in Kansas. He thought it would be different; with her so far away from Frank and all the support he had from her family.

Frank was there when Marty stepped off the train. He had no idea how happy she was to see him! It was so wonderful to be with Frank again after a week with her insane family! California looked like paradise!

Marty's entire family continued crucifying and harassing her to death about the divorce with telephone calls and letters. One day she received an envelope in the mail. She could tell by the postmark that it came from her oldest sister, Delorse, even though there was no return address. Inside, there was nothing but a pamphlet. The front of it had the flames of fire in Hell with big bold letters saying, "**YOU ARE GOING TO HELL!**" Marty started shaking so badly she had to sit down. She thought, "Delorse probably hasn't been off of her knees praying for my soul since I saw her on Christmas." Marty grew up in the

Assembly of God Church and was taught, "You are married by the Bible and divorced by the law. Divorce was an unforgivable mortal sin!" In Marty's family, the definition of marriage was, "*A life sentence without the possibility of parole!*"

Frank talked to his pastor about the hang-ups Marty had with divorce. She went to the Lutheran Church with Frank every week and Pastor Meese was wonderful to her. He kept telling her, "Grace, Marty, Grace; God forgives all sins." Marty would be fine, then she would get a call from someone in her family. Gib talked her into reconciliation, making grand promises that he would change and be a considerate and thoughtful husband. Frank understood her dilemma when she explained to him that she had to give it a shot. She didn't make it through the first evening. He tried to kiss her and she was out of there, and drove straight back to Frank! Marty told Frank, "There's no way I can live with this guy that I don't love or respect." It was so bad she couldn't stand the sight of him. Then her demons would return and she was back to square one. If she went through with the divorce and remarried, she would be living in sin. She was terrified of going to Hell. Her religious beliefs she grew up with were instilled in her.

Frank and Gib were still working together in the same office and in the same car pool. Gib didn't tell anyone at work that his wife had moved out and filed for divorce; it wouldn't have looked good for him. However, he did tell the car pool driver when they were alone. Gib also told him that a friend was dating his wife, but didn't say who. One morning, the driver quietly brought it up with Gib in the front seat when everyone else was in the back of the van. Frank was reading the newspaper, but heard every word. The driver said to Gib, "I wish I could get my hands on that bastard that is dating your wife." He had *no idea* that the "bastard" was sitting in the back seat of his van!

Early one morning, Marty's car wouldn't start and she called Frank. His apartment was just down the street from hers. He told her, "No problem, I'll call Jim and have him pick me up at your place and you can drive my car to work." When Frank got into the van, Jim asked, "Why are we picking you up at Marty's apartment?" Frank explained, "Her car wouldn't start this morning so she called to borrow mine." Looking totally confused, Jim asked, "But why would she call you?" *He was not the sharpest knife in the drawer.*

Marty started having a lot of stomach problems. She went to her doctor and they gave her an upper GI; she had ulcers. At work, Marty held her stomach with one hand while she wrote with the other. Her supervisor came over to her desk and asked if she needed some time off work. He could see that she was in a lot of pain. She just told him, "No, I can hurt here just as easy as I would at home."

Gib's mother, Charlotte, came to California for a visit. When Marty agreed to see her, Charlotte told her to *grow up*. She let Charlotte have it with both barrels, reminding her of all the crap she put up with, from her and Gib's dad. Then Marty wrapped it up by saying, "If you want to go around telling people to *grow up*; tell that to your son! While you are at it, tell your husband too!" (Marty was amazed on how fast Charlotte cooled down with that suggestion.) When Marty left, the kitchen window was open and she overheard Charlotte saying to Gib, "She has got to have some Indian blood in her. She never forgets a thing, does she?"

Butch and Judy came to California on vacation. Butch and Gib were close buddies in Kansas. Judy and Marty were close friends too. As usual, Butch was in control and Judy had no voice in making their plans. Marty wasn't even going to see her friend unless she agreed to make it a foursome, including Gib. Marty was a damn fool again, and played into Gib's hands with help from Butch. The four of them went to Sea World in San Diego for the day. Gib and Butch wanted to kill Judy when she said, "We can love you both as much apart as together." They returned from San Diego late that night.

Frank was royally pissed with Marty and told his parents about her little trip to San Diego. A couple of days later, Frank and Marty went over to his Mom and Dad's for the evening. Dad tore into Marty like a coyote after a rabbit. He was relentless,

calling her a whore and a slut! She tried to tell him she just
went for the day to be able to spend time with her friend Judy.
This bastard made Marty's Dad look like milk toast! Marty ran
in the bathroom in tears. Frank's Mom came in to talk to her
and comfort her. Frank and Marty left and went back to his
apartment. Marty got in her car and left immediately, sobbing
so hard that she could barely see to drive. She drove all over
on side streets and freeways, not knowing where she was or
where she was going, she just wanted to die. The only thing that
kept her from committing suicide was the fear of going to Hell.
There it was again, *going to Hell*. She ended up at the mobile
home, pounding on the door. It was past midnight and Gib was
in bed. He turned on a light and answered the door. When he
saw her face, he knew what had happened. She had a nervous
breakdown. Her eyes were vacant, no expression whatsoever!
Gib called Frank and asked him to meet them at the hospital.
They told Marty later that she signed herself into the hospital,
but she didn't remember it. Two weeks later, she was released and
went back to work. Pastor Meese and her psychiatrist helped
her tremendously, and she was on medication. Gib came to the
hospital to see her. He said, "I need to thank you for something.
If it wasn't for you, I would have spent the rest of my life rotting
in Kansas, working for my dad in that damn garage."

Frank's family came to the hospital to see her. Even Dad
came, but didn't speak to Marty except to say *hi and good-by*. He
just did his usual thing, sitting back and looking like a mad bull
dog with his arms folded across his chest.

When Marty had her twenty-fifth birthday, Frank sent
twenty-five beautiful, long-stemmed red roses to her at the
office. He had oatmeal for dinner every night with her for several
weeks, to heal her ulcers. She protested, saying it was no meal
for a man. He said, "If you can do it, so can I!" He was constantly
looking out for her and showered her with gifts. When she asked
what the occasion was, his reply would be, "Does it have to be
an occasion for me to buy something for my gal?" He took her to
lovely restaurants for dinner. They had so much fun just staying

home at his apartment and watching TV. This was a whole new world for Marty. She had never been treated like this by anyone in her life! Frank really cared! He was not only the love of her life, but also her best friend and sole mate.

CHAPTER TWENTY-TWO

When Frank and Marty went over to tell his parents, "We're getting married!" Dad said, "You have our blessing, but we're holding our breath!" Both of them just let it go and changed the subject. Marty was fully aware, that Frank's Dad was God and no one was allowed to stand up to him. Mom had everyone trained to walk on eggs around him.

Marty told Frank, "Before we can get married, you have to go back to Kansas with me and meet my family. I don't ever want you to be able to throw up to me that you had no idea what a crazy family you married into!"

They set up their vacations at the same time and drove straight through to Kansas, stopping only for gas and to eat. Frank had never been east of California. He was in his glory seeing the country. They were driving through New Mexico when the sun came up, and Frank thought it was the most beautiful sunrise he had ever seen. He noticed occasional road signs; *Speed limit 35*. He finally asked Marty, "Why are we slowing down?" She answered, "We are coming into a town." He looked around and asked, "A town, where?" There would be a gas station, a country store, and a few houses. Then he noticed a road sign; *DO NOT DRIVE ON SHOULDER*. He asked, "Why would anyone drive on the shoulder of the road?" Marty replied, "You'll see." Sure enough, a few miles down the road, a farmer was driving on the shoulder of the road with his tractor. Since he had been a city boy all of his life; Frank was totally fascinated with Marty's world in the country.

It was late in the afternoon when they arrived in Liberal, Kansas, and stopped to call Marty's Dad. He was working on a job not far from Liberal. When they were leaving California, he told them on the phone, "Call me when you get to Liberal and I will come meet you there, then you can follow me to Hays." Marty called the number her Dad had given her and they told her Howard was already there in Liberal at the chiropractor's office. Dad hurt his back again on the job. The chiropractor took x-rays and discovered a fracture in his back. After he fit Dad into a back brace, they checked into a motel and went to a café for dinner before retiring for the night. The next day, Marty drove her car to Hays with Dad lying down in the back seat, and Frank drove Dad's junky car full of materials and tools. As they drove through small towns, people occasionally waved to Frank because they recognized Dad's car, then did a double-take and gave Frank a funny look, obviously wondering who he was and what he was doing driving Howard's car. Dad knew people all over the central and southwest parts of Kansas from his wiring jobs. Frank was totally amazed! He was born and raised in the L.A. area where you didn't know all of the neighbors in your immediate neighborhood. This was a whole new world to him.

When they arrived in Hays, everyone in the family had come to see Marty and to meet the *city slicker* Frank. A couple of days later, it was Dad's night to bowl in his league. He was going with a fractured back and no one could talk him out of it. They set the clocks back and removed the distributor cap off of his car, but he called a bowling buddy to pick him up and slipped out the back door. Marty called the chiropractor in Liberal when they discovered he was gone. She asked, "Should Dad be bowling with his fractured back?" He replied, "Don't be ridiculous; he can't bowl with a fractured back." Marty said "Well, that's exactly what he's doing as we speak!" The doctor was so upset he started yelling, "One wrong move and he could paralyze himself for life! I can't believe Howard would be so stupid!" Frank and Marty got in the car immediately and went to the bowling alley to tell Dad what the doctor said, but he refused to quit, insisting that he would be just fine.

Frank showed real tolerance in meeting Marty's family. He got along great with Dad and Betty, even though he couldn't stand Betty. Delorse was the religious fanatic that condemned everything under the sun but eating, sleeping, and praying. Her husband, Earl, was an okay guy. As usual, Laura was very critical of Marty, and that went over like a lead balloon with Frank. Laura's husband, Estel, was rude and crude with a big cigar always hanging out of his mouth. Frank would have thought Byron was gay if he didn't have a wife and a little boy. Byron's wife, Bernice, was very religious and it was obvious that she was only there out of obligation. She was very uncomfortable around Laura and especially Estel. Marty loved all of her nephews and nieces. It was difficult to be so far away from them and not see them grow up.

After Frank and Marty got back from Kansas; Frank told his sister, "I want to surprise Marty with a small engagement party. It came up in conversation on our trip that she has never had a party in her life." Frank made reservations for ten people at a nice restaurant that had live music and dancing. Marty was caught completely off guard, and was thrilled when they arrived at the restaurant. She had no idea that tonight was going to enlighten her as to what her future sister-in-law was all about; a thoughtless, self-centered little brat. Frank gave Marge money to buy a corsage for Marty to have at the restaurant for when Frank and Marty arrived. Marge bought one for herself too! They were seated at a long table, away from the dance floor, in a private room. After dinner, Marge grabbed Frank to go to the dance floor. Everyone else followed, except Marty and Dad. They were there alone for quite awhile and Marty was extremely uncomfortable, feeling like a wallflower. Dad didn't speak to her; he just sat there drinking and puffing away on his damn pipe! Marge took over the entire party; running around, screaming and hollering.

Later, when they returned to the apartment, Marty told Frank, "I didn't appreciate being left alone so long with Dad." Frank replied, "It certainly wasn't fun for me either!" He removed the shoe and sock from his bad foot; his foot was bleeding from being on it too long on the dance floor. His sock was soaked with blood. Horrified at what his own sister had done to him, Marty asked, "What kind of a relationship do you have with your family that you couldn't say you were hurting and needed to sit down?"

Their families had a striking resemblance with the exception of Frank's Mom. Frank's family didn't concern themselves with his feelings or welfare anymore than Marty's family did for her. Marty knew even though Mom was sweet and wonderful to her, Marge was her baby girl. Frank had been brainwashed as a child, "Don't make your sister cry. Do whatever it takes to make your sister happy." Marge was treated like she was a delicate little flower.

When Frank was in college, he was in a horrible accident. He was a passenger in a car with a friend of his, who was drag racing when he lost control of the car, wiping out five trees. Frank was thrown out of the car for eighty-seven feet and landed on the pavement, head first. The driver walked away from the accident unharmed. The doctor told Frank's parents, "I give him three days to live." He was in a coma for ten weeks with a severe concussion. The calf was severely damaged in his left leg and the bone in his upper thigh was broken in three places. Then his left foot developed gangrene. They surgically tied two veins together to stop the gangrene from spreading and had to partially amputate his toes, making them stubs to save the foot and leg. He was in a body cast for over a year. The doctors told him he would never walk again without a brace. He hated the brace, and never stopped trying until he could walk without it. When he came home after being in the hospital for fourteen weeks, he was rushed back twenty-four hours later for an emergency appendectomy. His Mom was his nurse until he was back on his feet. He developed his own style of walking. The left Achilles tendon was frozen and the foot would not bend. When taking a step, he lifted the knee a little higher than normal and skipped. Marty thought it was cute and sexy. This is why Frank had so much understanding for Marty's back pain. He was no stranger to pain himself.

CHAPTER TWENTY-THREE

Frank and Marty planned a very small wedding in a beautiful wedding chapel in West Covina, *Little Chapel of Flowers*. They held the reception at the wedding chapel afterwards, serving only mints, nuts and wedding cake with champagne. They had lovely music and dancing.

Marty's Dad and her stepmother, Betty, arrived a week before the wedding on a train. Dad was good natured about it all, but Marty knew he was dead set against this wedding. He was concerned about what Frank's parents would think because he wasn't paying for it. Marty wanted to say, "You didn't pay for my first wedding, why would you pay for this one?" Instead, she just said, "They don't expect you to, since this is my second marriage."

The wedding was in the evening. All day long, Dad kidded her and said, "Look at those clouds, honey; it's going to pour down buckets tonight on your wedding!" Marty kept saying, "No Dad, it doesn't rain like that here. It rains in the winter for days at a time, but it comes down nice and easy." Dad replied, "I hate to tell you this, but that's not the way it will be tonight!" They went early, so Marty could dress in the bridal room. After they had arrived and just barely made it inside the door, the rain came down in buckets just as Dad predicted. Many streets were flooded, and people had to take different routes to get there. Other than family, only a few friends were invited with thirty people in all. Dad and Betty were the only members of Marty's family there. Marty was thankful the rest of her family couldn't afford to come; everyone would have thought *The Beverly Hillbillies* had arrived on the scene. The wedding started forty-five minutes late because of the rain. They had hired a friend who went to their church to sing. He arrived in his construction clothes, soaked to the skin, with mud almost to the top of his boots. He changed into his tux and dress shoes at the chapel. Marty's friend who was going to handle the guest book had to take a detour to get there, and arrived later than most of the guests. Frank's cousin, Annette, stepped in for the job.

There was so much chaos; they could have made a sitcom out of it. Marty was getting very nervous and warm in the bridal room. After everyone had finally arrived and they said the ceremony would start, her nose started bleeding. Marge ran out yelling, "Not yet! We have a problem!" Marty got the bleeding to stop, but had a handkerchief in her hand under the bridal bouquet just in case it started again. As Dad and Marty started down the aisle, he said to her with a smile on his face, "How many times do I have to give you away?" Marty smiled back at him and said, "This is it, Dad. This time, it's forever!" While Frank and Marty were saying their vows, she was still warm and feeling dizzy. The minister kept saying softly in between the vows, "Deep breaths, Marty, deep breaths." After the wedding, pastor laughed and said to Marty, "I thought we were going to lose you there for a few minutes." Marty smiled and thought to herself, "I was very nervous, but this time I didn't want to run for my life! This time, I have a wonderful guy who really cares! He is my lover, my best friend, and my soul mate!"

When it was time for the bride and groom to leave the chapel, the rain had stopped. They were showered with rice as they made a mad dash to the car. Then they were off to fabulous Las Vegas for their honeymoon!

It was very late when they arrived in Barstow, so they got a nice room there. Marty changed into her beautiful lingerie in the bathroom. When she came out, Frank had a cold bottle of champagne with two champagne glasses. He never ceased to amaze Marty with his thoughtfulness. However, after they had a couple of glasses, Marty passed out cold! Frank thought, "Well, so much for the wedding night!"

When Marty woke up the next morning, she couldn't believe what she had done and apologized profoundly, but Frank said, "Its okay, Babe, we have the rest of our lives." They drove on to Vegas and checked into the Sands. It was a beautiful place! They made up for the night in Barstow, big time! After staying at the Sands for a couple of nights, they moved to the Hacienda for the next two nights. It was the new place in town and really lovely.

It was the first time for both of them to *do Vegas*. Marty loved all the lights, the action, and night life! They saw the *Ink Spots* at a lounge show and they were terrific! In 1967, there were fantastic lounge shows in all the big casinos. No cover charge, just buy a drink and enjoy the show. The Follies Bergere at the Tropicana was a fabulous Vegas show! Their costumes were gorgeous as well as the girls! It really didn't bug Marty that they were topless; the show wasn't presented as a sexy production. The show girls were all very graceful in a form of art, tall and thin. Marty said to Frank, "I had more boobs than that when I was thirteen." He laughed and replied, "I don't doubt that for a minute!" He had teased her many times about her boobs saying, "I always say anything over a handful is a waste and you are certainly a handful!"

They also went to see Jimmy Rodgers and Rosemary Clooney. When they were in the showroom waiting for the Rosemary Clooney show to start, Marty noticed a gal sitting in front, chatting with friends. She commented to Frank, "She sure is a cute and bubbly gal." Later during the show, Rosemary introduced her. It was Connie Stevens! This little country gal was star struck.

All the food was wonderful and they ate like kings! It took Marty about two minutes to become completely hooked on the nickel slots. (Marty gave Frank a bad time about his football bets. She was raised that gambling was wrong, a tool of the devil himself! So Frank brought her to Vegas and corrupted his little country gal from the Bible belt. He never heard anything about his football bets again.) The slot machines were very simple then. They just had three reels with cherries, oranges, watermelons, and lemons with only one line. No special affects or animation. No buttons to push, you had to pull the handle. The coins had to be hand fed into the machine; they didn't take bills or tickets. Frank and Marty allowed themselves ten dollars a day to gamble, one nickel at a time, and had a ball! What a town! It was the most exciting place on earth! They had the best time of their lives!

CHAPTER TWENTY-FOUR

Frank and Marty came home to a new apartment. It was very nice with a large living room. They combined everything from their two apartments and moved into it three weeks before their wedding. Marty lived in the new apartment and Frank stayed with his parents until the big day. The three weeks seemed to drag for both of them. Frank had to go home every night. If he didn't, Mom would have had a cow!

When the holidays arrived, they had so much fun putting up their first Christmas tree together. Early on Christmas Eve, Frank and Marty opened their gifts to each other. She bought Frank some new clothes. He surprised her with ten new dresses for work and also a beautiful corsage for her to wear to church and to the Christmas Eve party that night at Mom and Dad's. Mom served a wonderful buffet, and there were many lovely gifts she had bought at Nash's for everyone, under the gorgeous Christmas tree. Mom was the office manager at Nash's, a department store with top quality merchandise.

Dad made a point to tell Frank in Marty's presence, "You have set a hell of precedent buying her all that for Christmas! Boy, are you stupid!" (Mom bought her own presents from Dad and wrapped them herself to put under the tree. Dad never helped her with any of the housework, even though she worked full time.)

Frank loved to help Marty. When she was in the kitchen cleaning up after dinner, he was right there. This was a brand-new thing for Marty; she never had help from her Dad or Gib. Quite to the contrary, she waited on them hand and foot. However, when Frank and Marty had dinner guests, it embarrassed her that he was right there after dinner, helping with the clean up, until some friends told her she was nuts! They said, "If he wants to help, let him! Sit down and enjoy it!" After that, clean-up was his baby! Frank didn't make any points with the guys though, when their wives gave them the elbow and said, "Watch Frank and learn!"

Now that Frank and Marty were married, Marge and Dick saw them as fair game to bug them to death. They only lived six blocks away and were pounding on their door at 8:00 a.m. every Saturday morning. Marge and Dick did not enter a room, they would attack it! They waltzed in like it was a drunken party, yelling and screaming! Since Frank and Marty both worked full time and went to church on Sunday, Saturday was their day. They liked to sleep in and make love before tackling their Saturday chores. Many times, Marge and Dick would be pounding on their front door when Frank and Marty were still in bed doing the rumba. Finally, Marty said to Frank, "You need to talk to your sister and tell her the facts of life. Don't just drop in, call first." It all went down hill from there really fast. No one could tell Marge and Dick what they could or could not do except Dad. Dick had a drinking problem. Marty never saw him without a drink in his hand. Marty had no problem with people having a drink occasionally, but had a real problem with Dick's drinking. Mom and Dad told her to let the booze flow freely for Dick just to keep him happy. In fact, they expected Frank and Marty to do anything and everything to keep both Marge and Dick happy, to keep the peace in the family.

Frank came home from work one day and told Marty, "I have some really bad news. Mobil Oil is moving their entire accounting department to Dallas. We have to move to Texas or I'm out of a job, and I don't want to leave California." Marty was relieved and said to him, "This is great, honey! You can just get another job here and Gib will be completely out of our life once and for all!" (Frank was still working with Gib in the same office.) He was worried about finding another job. Marty reassured him,

"You will have no problem at all!" Frank found a job very soon, with Frigidaire on the order desk, working with the Frigidaire dealers. They made many new friends and it opened up a whole new world for them.

CHAPTER TWENTY-FIVE

A few months later, Marty was three weeks late with her period and went to her doctor. He examined her and said, "I think you are pregnant, but we'll know for sure when the test comes back. Frank and Marty were so excited! She said to Frank that night, "Let's go to Nash's and look at baby things." Frank said, "We don't even know for sure yet, let's wait." Marty insisted, "I'm not saying I want to buy anything, I just want to have fun looking." So after dinner they went to Nash's and Marty was having a ball, she was so happy!

While they were looking at all the cute little baby things, a guy walked up to them and said cautiously, "Hi Frank, how are you?" Frank just looked at him, giving him a stare before he spoke, "I'm fine, how are you?" Marty didn't know who this guy was, but you could have cut the air with a knife it was so thick! Frank introduced him to Marty. They chatted for a few minutes, and then the guy was gone. Frank turned to Marty and said, "That was him!" Marty asked, "That was who?" Then it hit her, and she said, "That was the guy driving the car when you had your accident!" Frank said, "Yep! The one and only! This is the first time I've seen him since the night of the accident! He never came to see me, not one time! My family saw him many times in the corridor of the hospital on my floor, but that's as far as he got, he could not come into my room." Marty said, "I think I would rather be in your shoes than his, Babe. He's still going through a private hell mentally, sailing on a royal guilt trip, and it's been eight years since your accident." Frank just looked at her, thinking about what she said, and replied, "I never thought of it that way."

Marty called the doctor's office a few days later and the test came back negative. She was disappointed, but Mom reassured her, "Don't worry honey, you'll get pregnant."

Marge and Dick were looking for a house and asked Frank and Marty to go with them on Sunday afternoons. They sold their first house and were renting temporarily. Marge told Marty the story of when she was pregnant with Melody, their firstborn. She had complications and was bedridden for awhile, when they were right in the middle of moving into their first house. It had been a nightmare for Marge. Marty got to thinking about it and realized that could happen to her. She had already been told by doctors that carrying a baby through nine months of pregnancy was going to be difficult for her with her back and hips. So Marty really got into the house-hunting with Marge and Dick. Frank said, "Let's wait until you are pregnant before buying a house." Marty argued, "I don't want to go through what Marge did with Melody. The doctors have already told me that carrying a child will be extremely painful for me. I don't want to move into a house and have the work of getting settled while I am pregnant. Our apartment complex does not allow children, so we would have to move before the baby was born." Frank was not convinced that he even wanted a house with his bad leg and Marty's back problems. He wasn't even sure he wanted Marty pregnant. He was always so damn practical! Marty hated being practical—she had her dreams! Frank was like a mother hen to Marty when it came to her health and welfare.

Marty was between jobs at the time. Frank and Mom had convinced her to quit her job at Euclid. The work load was heavy and difficult with her back. She was going to her chiropractor two or three times a week. The muscles in her shoulders were so tight all the time; they were hard as rocks.

Money was not a problem, so Marty was dragging her feet on getting another job. Her heart wasn't in it. They had no debts, and the rent on their apartment was only one hundred and thirty-eight dollars a month. Frank had a savings account with well over eleven thousand dollars in it; a lot of money in 1968 for a young couple just starting out in life.

Frank started mowing lawns in his neighborhood when he was nine years old. When he turned fourteen, he started working at the local Safeway grocery store as a box boy. By the time he graduated from college, he was assistant manager of the store, working forty hours a week while going to college full-time, beating the hell out of his bad leg. He had true grit! He lived at home with his parents. Instead of just blowing his money, like most kids, he only allowed himself so much for his car, dating and having fun. Every payday, he made a deposit into his savings account and made do with what was left.

Since Marty was not working, she started house hunting during the week while Frank was at work. She soon realized they couldn't afford a nice house in the Arcadia area where Frank grew up and where his parents still lived. Arcadia was a very expensive area. Marty started working with a team of realtors and began looking in Covina where real estate was less expensive and you got much more for your money.

Marty had not found anything that really grabbed her; then the realtors took her to a house in Glendora, a lovely area about fifteen miles east of Arcadia. Before Marty got out of the car she knew—this is it! Her dream house! It had double front doors leading into a large atrium and the entire house was built in a U-shape around it. When entering the atrium, on your right was a sliding glass door to the living room. In front of you, was a large solid wall of glass with another sliding glass door to enter the family room. The beautiful patio and back yard could be seen through the family room that had another sliding glass door on the other side of the room. A sliding glass door in the large master bedroom went out to the Japanese tea garden. The garden had a wood decking and fish pond. There were high cathedral ceilings throughout the house with high windows in addition to the lower windows. In the back yard, there was a view of hills and mountains. It had a large yard in front as well as in the back, beautifully landscaped. The house was 1,850 square feet, not counting the large atrium or the oversized two-car garage attached to the house.

Marty called Frank and asked him to come to the real estate office directly from work. He was not happy, to say the very least, but he came to meet Marty and the two realtors. When they took him to see the house, he said, "I don't even understand why you want this house. All I see is work with all that glass to clean." Marty wouldn't give up; she had to have this house or die! She promised him, "If we buy this house, you will never clean a window or glass door, I will do it myself." Frank wanted to show it to Dad before he gave them a deposit. Marty argued, "Your father is not going to live here, we are! You don't need his approval!" They were asking twenty-seven thousand five hundred dollars. Frank made them an offer of twenty-five thousand five hundred dollars, not dreaming they would accept it. The realtors called at 1:00 a.m. to tell them, "You have just bought your first house! They accepted your offer!" After Frank hung up, he yelled at Marty, "I hope you are happy! We bought a house! What the hell are we going to do with a house?"

The next day was the fourth of July, and they were going to Marge and Dick's for a family barbecue. When Frank and Marty arrived, they found everyone sitting in the back yard having drinks and snacks. They didn't say anything about the house until after all the greetings and they sat down with their drinks. Then they calmly stated, "We bought a house last night." Everyone screamed at once, "You did what?" Dad started yelling at Frank, "What did you do a dumb thing like that for? You should have had me check into it first. What an idiot! You don't make moves like that without discussing it with me! Where is this damn house anyway?"

The next day, the whole family went with the realtors to see the house. The owners were in Las Vegas for three days, but the realtors had a key. Dad went through the entire house and back yard. He started smiling and said, "You have made a damn good investment here. I can't believe the price you got it for; its worth much more than that." Mom loved it! She thought it was beautiful! After Frank had his Dad's approval, he was full of excitement too! Marge and Dick wanted to shit—they were livid!

Marge and Dick stepped up their efforts to find a house. One night, the phone rang after Frank and Marty were in bed. It was Marge making her big announcement, "We bought a house! It's at the end of a cul-de-sac on a pie-shaped lot. It has a detached garage. There are railroad tracks behind the property. The house is smaller than what we need, but it's all we can afford in this area. We had to buy in this area because we have to be near the folks. But we'll be moving in two weeks, so we will be in our house before you get into yours! Tee hee. We'll be in our house first!" Frank and Marty told her, "That's great! Congratulations!" They hung up and started laughing. Marty said, "She sounded just like a little kid; tee hee, ha ha, me first! Who in the hell cares who moves in first? That is so childish and stupid." Frank asked Marty, "Did you notice that she didn't say one word about what she liked about the house? All you heard is what she didn't like! The only reason they bought that house is because it's ready to move into now, so they can move in first. Boy, is that stupid or what?"

Dick belittled Marty constantly, making fun of the way she talked. Marty's Dad mispronounced words, and some of it had rubbed off on Marty. The "Kansas twang" was a factor too. There was a definite difference in the way some words were pronounced in Kansas versus California. Frank helped her with pronunciations and she improved a lot, but Dick still loved to antagonize her. It got to the point that Marty didn't want to open her mouth around Dick. He would sit on the edge of his chair across from her and watch her when she was talking, with a shit ass grin on his face, just waiting for her to mispronounce a word. Sometimes he jumped on what she said when she had actually said it correctly. If anyone did that to precious little Marge, she would have been in tears.

After moving and getting settled in their house, Marty's stomach problems returned and she had a lot more pain in her back and neck. She got a job and had started working again before they moved into the house. There were many times she would get to bed after midnight and was up at six in the morning. Even with a lot of help from Frank, she was killing herself doing the cooking, cleaning, laundry, yard work, plus working in the office too. Her standard working hours in the office were forty-four hours a week. She had to work every Saturday morning.

Frank insisted that she see her doctor, and went with her. The doctor told Frank, "It's too stressful for Marty to be working with her stomach and back problems." After they walked out of the doctor's office, Frank said to Marty, "We can't *make* it on my salary!" Marty retorted, "Yes we can! You are forgetting that this house is going to give us a big tax break. The house payment is going to remain the same, but your salary will continue to go up. We also won't have the expense of my working; car gas, clothes, and dry cleaning. We'll be just fine!" Marty still kept a budget and watched it very closely. She always knew exactly where they were for the entire year with income minus expenses.

CHAPTER TWENTY-SIX

When Frank and Marty moved into their house, she knew very little about California gardening which was completely different from the Mid-West. Mom taught her a lot, showing her what to do and how to do it. She said it brought back a lot of memories of when they were still in their house. They moved into a beautiful condo when Frank was still in college.

Uncle Frank, Dad's brother, was his only sibling. He and Aunt Rose lived in Arcadia, in a beautiful house on one-third of an acre. He had three hundred and fifty rose bushes, with their identifications on small metal plates in front of each bush. There were many Uncle Frank had bred and named himself. He gave Marty some slips from his rose bushes. Mom and Marty put the slips in sand and water with B1, and nursed them along until they were ready to plant. Every time they were on the phone Mom asked, "How's our babies doing?" When Mom and Dad came once a week for dinner, Mom would head straight out to the rose bushes. Those *babies* grew to be five feet tall!

Mom showed Marty how to paint, and they painted the wooden strips between the cement squares in the atrium and on the patio. They had a ball! Marty was also busy decorating the interior of the house. When Frank would object to what she was spending, Dad stood up for her, saying, "Leave her alone, she does a great job!" Marty went to great lengths to buy really nice things that were on sale and was good at improvising.

Dad and Betty drove out from Kansas for a visit. Dad brought materials and tools with him to do projects on Frank and Marty's house. He put in a sprinkler system and Malibu lights in the yard; dishwasher in the kitchen; sink in the garage; and a fire circle in the atrium. Dad and Betty arrived just in time for the first Thanksgiving dinner in their home. Frank's family, including Dick's parents, came with Marge and Dick in their station wagon. Marty discovered where Dick got his rudeness. His Mother criticized Marty for everything under the sun that day. Frank's Mom knew Marty had killed herself making the house, yard, and dinner absolutely perfect. She told Marty when they were alone in the kitchen, "Don't let her get to you honey, everything is wonderful." Then Mom laughed and said, "You should have heard the conversation in the car today on the way out here. Dick said to his parents several times, *'Now remember, out here you get a lot more for your money. We couldn't move out of the area because we have to be near our parents.'*" Dick made several digs that day about Frank and Marty moving out to the sticks, when actually, they were surrounded by city. After he said it a few times, Mom jumped all over him saying, "Oh, that's what they all said when we moved to Arcadia from L.A. in 1937. Arcadia was out in the middle of nowhere, surrounded by desert. Now look at it, it's a big city surrounded by other cities."

Everyone was sitting on the patio when Marty told them about a snake she had seen recently in the back yard. Marge said, "When we were in our first house, I was in the front yard weeding one day and saw a snake on the driveway by Melody, who was a baby at the time in the stroller. I ran into the house screaming, and left my baby out there alone with the snake!" Melody spoke up and asked, "Mom! How could you do that to me?" Marge just laughed. Marty thought to herself, "I knew she was selfish, but this is unbelievable! She cared more about herself than her precious little baby!"

After the first of the year, Marty received a call from her Dad. Betty kicked him out and he was staying with friends. He could not afford to pay for the divorce, so Frank and Marty paid for it. Frank said it was money well spent, he couldn't stand Betty. Dad found out about Marty's ex-father-in-law screwing around with Betty when Dad was out of town. He also heard that one of their neighbors came across the alley when he saw

Dad leave town on a job. Dad couldn't believe it! (Marty never let on to her Dad that she knew all about it before she moved to California.)

After the divorce was filed, Dad moved into Grandma's house in Larned. Grandma lived with Aunt Lula and Uncle Guy because her health and eyesight had failed to a point that she couldn't be alone. Marty was shocked when her Grandma said to her, "I'm so glad Howard is rid of Betty. She was nothing but an old whore." *Marty didn't know her Grandma even knew that word!*

When the holidays came, Marty sent her Dad a plane ticket. One day at the breakfast table, he told her, "I would have never married Betty if it wasn't for you. I wanted to back out, but felt I couldn't because you were already living with her before our wedding." Marty replied, "Well, I wouldn't have married Gib if it wasn't for you. I wanted to kiss him off many times, and you would talk me out of it. You kept telling me that he was one fine guy!" Dad just smiled and said, "Well, I guess that makes us even then, doesn't it?"

Marty was still unable to get pregnant, and decided to take fertility tests. The results showed that Frank was sterile and it didn't look likely that Marty could conceive either. In the process of all these tests, Marty had to take in Frank's sperm to be checked. She had to get it to the lab within two hours and hold the bottle under her arm pit until she got there to keep it warm. This was no small feat. They only had one car at the time, so Marty had to drive Frank to work thirty miles one way and back in the middle of rush hour. They couldn't drop it off before Frank went to work because the lab wasn't open yet. She got back and found the address her doctor gave her and rushed it in just in time. The waiting room was packed with people. Marty went up to the desk and said softly, "I have my husband's sperm." The lady gave her a funny look and asked, "You have what?" Marty said a little louder, "I brought in my husband's sperm to be tested." Everyone in the room started snickering. Marty wanted to disappear into the woodwork! The lady said to her, "You're in the wrong place honey, this is an optometry office." Marty could hear everyone cracking up; after she made an exit faster than a speeding bullet!

They discussed adopting, but Frank wanted no part of it. It was 1970, the hippy years, and he was afraid they would get a baby from a mother who had smoked pot or taken drugs while she was pregnant. Marty was having a lot of difficulty dealing with it. One day, she was in the grocery store with a cart full of food when she saw a lady with her little baby. Marty couldn't hold back the tears. She walked out of the store, leaving the cart full of food and went home. She needed a baby to love. There was a void in her heart that only motherhood could fill.

Marty went into the pet store one day to buy some more tropical fish for her two aquariums. There were two poodle puppies there. She picked one of them up and couldn't put him down. She bought him and everything she needed for him; a doggy dish, collar, leash, and puppy food.

Frank came home that night from work and saw the dish on the floor in the kitchen. Marty didn't hear him come in the door. He made an announcement of his observation, "There's an animal in this house! Where is it and what is it?" The puppy heard this and thought, "Oh, oh! I've got my work cut out for me." It didn't take two minutes for him to steal Daddy's heart, big time! He was Daddy's boy. They were a family! Buttons kept them entertained constantly—he was a born ham!

One Saturday, Frank and Marty were on the San Bernardino Freeway when traffic came to a sudden stop. A camper lost its brakes going sixty-five miles per hour and hit the car in front of it, causing that car to spin completely around. The car hit Frank and Marty's car in the process, hit another car and shoved it into yet another car, and then hit the center divider. Five vehicles in all were involved. Frank and Marty were taken to the hospital by ambulance. Frank had a fractured vertebrate and Marty had severe whip lash. It was so severe that the doctor said it was a fine line between her having whip lash and a broken neck. Frank was flat on his back in the hospital for eight days, until the brace came in that was special-ordered for him. Marty was given pain medication with a whiplash collar and released. Mom and Dad came to the hospital and took Marty to the savage yard to pick up their car. The back end was badly damaged, but Marty was able to drive it to the body shop.

The next day, Marty thought her head was going to explode from the pain. Her doctor sent her to a therapist to have extensive physical therapy and eventually gave her shots in the back of her head to give her relief from the pain. Frank had physical therapy too after he was out of his back brace three months later. The guys at the office asked Frank, "How's your sex life with all of this Frank?" He replied, "I have to tie a string around it to remember what it's for!" The driver of the camper, who was at fault, did not have any insurance. After a few months, Frank and Marty's own car insurance cut them off, and they drained their savings account to pay for their medical bills, in addition to having the expense of a cleaning lady and gardener every week for several months.

One week after the accident, Dad and Mom were coming out to the house after visiting Frank in the hospital, so Dad could mow the lawn for Marty. Marge told Mom, "The girls and I want to come too." The second they walked into the house Marge was yelling, "What's for lunch? We haven't had lunch!" Marty said, "I don't know what I've got, I haven't been to the store. I've been eating at the hospital everyday." Marge pulled out cheese, bread, and butter and made grilled cheese sandwiches for everyone, turning Marty's kitchen into a total disaster. After lunch, Marge announced it was time to go. Mom yelled at Marge, "We are not going anywhere until we clean up this kitchen and leave it the way we found it! We came out here to help, not create more work for Marty!" Marty had never seen Mom raise her voice to Marge, but that day she lost it. It was difficult for Marty to keep a straight face—she wanted to crack up!

Marty had kept her promise to Frank that he would never have to clean a window or glass door if they bought that house. However, now she couldn't do what she did before the accident. She suffered terribly with migraine headaches and pain, with permanent damage in her neck and left shoulder. Frank also worried about her being on the nine-foot ladder, cleaning all the high windows every six weeks. They talked to a neighbor who said she had a great guy, Dale, do her windows. Frank told Marty to call Dale and set up a date. Dale and his helper did a fantastic job in two hours for only eight dollars. It took Marty three days to do all the windows and glass doors, inside and out, because she had to take so many breaks to rest because of the pain in her neck and back. Frank said to her, "I don't want you to ever touch these windows and doors again. We'll have Dale do them."

Six months later, Delorse and Earl got a divorce. Marty's divorce was the first in the history of the family, then Dad's divorce from Betty, and now Delorse. The family accused Marty of starting an epidemic. Delorse was a religious fanatic. When her children were small, she left them unattended without feeding them, and went to church while Earl was at work. Her housekeeping was beyond disgusting! Earl received full custody of all three children who were thirteen, fifteen, and seventeen years old at the time of the divorce.

Dad came to California for his annual visit a few months later. One day at the breakfast table, Dad started in about the divorce and was blaming Earl for everything, when it was a fact that Delorse had been a rotten wife and mother. Dad never liked Earl because of the elopement, which would have never happened without Laura's help, but Dad never acknowledged that fact. Marty told him, "When I stayed with them for two weeks every summer when I was in high school, Earl was a perfect gentleman. The time I went there to help Delorse when Tommy was so sick and in the hospital, I had no problem being in the house alone with Earl. Delorse was at the hospital around the clock with Tommy because he was just a baby. I cooked, washed dishes, cleaned house, did the laundry, and caught up on all the ironing while I took care of Vernon, who was three years old at the time. Earl appreciated everything I did very much. He didn't drink, smoke, cuss, or ever do anything improper to me. Estel, on the other hand, is a filthy and disgusting excuse for a man, yet you think he is great! You have bent over backwards to help Laura and Estel over the years, never doing shit for

Delorse and Earl! Estel drinks like a fish, he always has that stinking cigar hanging out of his mouth, his language would make a sailor blush, and he has a filthy mind! I'm going to tell you something I swore I would never tell anyone! That asshole molested and raped me again and again when they were living in our back yard in their trailer! He snuck up to my bedroom whenever no one was looking! I was terrified of screaming or telling anyone. I begged him to leave me alone! He would just stand there, laughing and sneering at me!" Dad just sat there a few minutes and didn't say a word. Then finally he said, "*You haven't said anything all these years, I don't know why you couldn't have kept this to yourself and not burdened me with it.*" Marty's eyes snapped with pure hatred! She said, "Thank you very much! You just refortified my reasoning for keeping my mouth shut at the time! I knew you and Laura would have blamed me! I was right! You're blaming me now and I am an adult! I hate to even think how I would have been treated if I had opened my mouth then! I would have been just like a trapped animal, taking anything you and Laura dished out!" Dad looked down his nose, got up, and left the kitchen table to go watch TV. Marty sat there and thought about what had just taken place. It didn't make a damn bit of sense that Dad showed no reaction of shock to what she had just told him. Then it hit her! *Son of a bitch!* She thought, "Dad and Laura both knew what was going on and turned their heads the other way so they didn't have to deal with it! That's why they constantly criticized me, ridiculed me and treated me like shit! They were both trying to relieve their own damn conscience by blaming me! My own father and sister sold me out!"

Less than thirty minutes later, Dad acted perfectly normal, as if the conversation didn't take place. He wiped it clean from his mind! Selective memory!

After Frank came home from work, they had dinner and watched TV. When they went to bed, he asked, "What's wrong, Babe? You haven't been yourself tonight." Marty told him what had transpired that day. (Marty had already told Frank all about Estel some time ago, so he knew all about it.) Frank didn't know how her Dad could say something that was so cruel. He didn't know that was the norm for Dad. As usual, Dad was just thinking of himself. A few days later, it was time for Dad to fly home and none too soon for Marty.

CHAPTER TWENTY-SEVEN

Early one morning, Frank and Marty suddenly came out of a deep sleep with the bed doing a dance on its own. Buttons snuggled up to Mom for protection. They were having an earthquake. It was about forty-five seconds long, but it seemed a lot longer with everything around you rocking and rolling. The bedroom drapes of the sliding glass door were open and they watched their back yard roll like gentle ocean waves. After it was over, Marty got up and made a check around the house. Many things were moved out of place, but nothing was broken. There were a few cracks in the stucco outside, plus a few cracks in the shower tiles in the master bath, but that was it. Frank got ready for work and Marty went back to sleep.

Later that morning, Lyn called from next door and announced it was coffee klatch time. She asked Marty, "Would you like a shot of bourbon in your coffee this morning?" Marty laughed and said, "Oh yeah! That was quite a shaker alright!" When she walked in next door, Lyn had the TV on, showing pictures of massive destruction. Marty asked, "What's that all about?" She replied, "Where were you this morning?" Marty's eyes went wide open in disbelief, "You mean to tell me that the earthquake did all that? Where?" Lyn said, "In Sylmar up in San Fernando Valley! The VA Hospital collapsed! Many people have died and they don't know how many are still trapped!"

A few days later, Frank came home and announced, "I just got laid off!" California was in a recession and he was low man in seniority. This was the second time Frank had been laid off in two years.

Byron, Bernice, Brent, and Beth drove out from Wichita, Kansas on vacation. Brent was five years old and Beth was eight months. She was a beautiful little doll, always laughing. Byron and Bernice couldn't afford to do a lot and Frank still didn't have a job, but they did go to Disneyland and had a great time.

Frank got a job with Bechtel Engineering through Dick, who was a personal friend. They had been friends for twenty years. Dick trained him on the job, and Frank was doing very well as a *Cost Engineer*.

Dick and Frank went to San Francisco on business to make a presentation to the Executive Board of Directors. This is where the home office was for Bechtel, where it all started for the Bechtel family. Dick's wife, Joanne, and Marty went too and did their own thing. They stayed at a gorgeous hotel, dined at lovely restaurants and had a ball!

Frank was on an elevator in the Bechtel building in downtown San Francisco, when a business colleague asked Frank how they were running on their overhead in the Norwalk Division of Southern California. Frank answered, "We're running over several million dollars, but what the hell, it's only Steve's money." The elevator door opened and someone said as they stepped in, "Hello Mr. Bechtel, how are you?" Frank turned around and there stood Steve Bechtel, Jr. right behind him, grinning from ear to ear, looking straight at him. Frank wanted to sink to the bottom of the elevator shaft!

They stayed over that week-end, took the ferry over to Tiburon and went to Sam's for breakfast. Even though it seemed like a crazy thing to do, they did what everyone else did at Sam's—had a gin fizz with their breakfast. They made a gin fizz like no one else on earth! Marty fell in love with San Francisco! It was completely different than when she came here with Gib five years ago, the point in time when she realized her marriage with Gib had died.

Vernon, Delorse's oldest son, and Joann got married and had a baby boy a few months later. He was only eighteen years old and had no way to support them, so he joined the Army. Frank and Marty drove up to Monterey to see him after his boot training at Fort Ord. They drove all over the area to take in the beautiful scenery and took Vernon to a lovely restaurant for dinner. Shortly after that, Vernon went back to Kansas on leave, to bring out his wife, Joann, and Buddy. Vernon called Marty to ask if Joann and Buddy could stay with them until he found an apartment. She answered, "Of course!"

When they arrived from Kansas, Frank couldn't believe they had made it in their junky car. He took Marty a side and said, "We've got to go down and find him a car. There's no way he's going to make it to Fort Ord in that wreck as bad as the rods are knocking." Frank had a friend who was a car salesman and he found them a good used car. Frank co-signed for Vernon on the car loan. When they got back to the house, Vernon thanked Frank with tears in his eyes. He said, "I asked Dad and Mom for their help to buy a better car before we left Kansas, but neither one of them would sign for me. You guys were there for us when we had no one else, I'll never forget this!" Frank said, "You are family Vernon, I was happy to do it." Joann and Buddy stayed with Frank and Marty for several weeks. Vernon came down from Fort Ord on the weekends he was off duty.

Marty was a little concerned that Buttons would be jealous of Buddy, but it was the other way around. Buttons was Buddy's little protector. When Buddy woke up from his nap in Joann's bedroom, where his crib was, Buttons wouldn't let Joann or Marty have a moment's peace until they brought Buddy out to the family room. Buttons would go to the doorway of the hall and dance around as if he was saying, "Come on! The baby is awake!" Vernon found a place and moved his little family up north, by Fort Ord, but they came down to Frank and Marty's a lot on weekends.

They came down when Frank and Marty had a "sleep over" party to bring in the New Year. Everyone spent the evening playing cards, eating and drinking. At midnight, they all toasted with champagne. There were five couples and three babies. They had a crib in each bedroom. All three babies were really good and there were no problems. The couple without a baby camped out on the carpet in the family room. Marty put down blankets, sheets and pillows for them with a fire in the fireplace. Frank, Marty, and Buttons slept on the sofas in the living room. Buttons kept them awake by sofa hopping, because he couldn't decide who he wanted to sleep with, Mom or Dad. He was used to the three of them being together in their king-sized bed. The next morning, they had sweet rolls, eggs, bacon and coffee for everyone. They spent the day watching the Rose Parade and Bowl games, stuffing themselves with more food and drink. Everyone said it was the best New Year they ever had except everyone gained five pounds from all the food.

Two weeks later, Vernon got his orders for Vietnam. They came down to spend a few days with Frank and Marty on their way to Kansas. Vernon took Joann and Buddy back to stay with her parents. Marty sobbed her heart out. She was losing *her kids* and was terrified of Vernon getting killed in Vietnam.

CHAPTER TWENTY-EIGHT

The day after Thanksgiving, Marty received a call from her brother, Byron. Marty couldn't understand him. He kept saying, "Bernice and Beth are gone." Bernice, Brent, little Beth, and Bernice's sister, Alma, drove to Great Bend to spend Thanksgiving with Bernice and Alma's parents. Byron didn't go because he had to work. On Friday morning when they were driving back to Wichita, it started to snow just outside of Great Bend. Bernice was meeting a semi-truck on a two-way highway when a car pulled out to pass the truck. Bernice was going to hit the car head on and slammed on her brakes. She fishtailed right into the path of the truck. The driver in the car, who caused the accident by passing the truck, took the ditch on the other side of the road and was not hurt. The truck rolled over into the field, but the driver was okay. Bernice and little Beth were killed instantly. Alma was severely bruised all over her body, but would be okay. Brent was thrown out of the car and found wondering around in the middle of the highway, trying to walk on a broken leg.

Marty couldn't believe it. She told Byron, "I'll fly in today, are you still in Wichita?" He said, "Yes." Then it dawned on her, "Wait a minute, you don't want to wait for me to fly in, I'm sure you want to get to Great Bend as fast as you can get there." He said, "No, I'm not going anywhere until you get here. I can't face this without you." She called the airlines right away and told them she needed to get the next flight out of LAX, and why. They said, "Don't worry, you tell us how soon you can get here and we'll make room for you on a flight." Then she called Frank at work and he came home immediately. The next call was to Lyn, her friend next door. She was at the front door before Marty hardly had time to hang up the phone. After they had their hugs and tears, Marty started pulling clothes out of the closet and Lyn helped her pack. Marty said, "Little baby Beth is gone. Bernice is gone. How is my brother going to survive this tragedy? Bernice took care of everything. She spoiled Byron rotten! There's no way my brother is going to survive losing Beth. He worshipped the ground she walked on! Beth is two and a half years old now. I just talked to her recently on the phone and started crying because she sounded so grown-up. I was crying because she was growing up too fast. My God! Now she's gone! And Brent! He is going to grow up without his mother just like we did!" Frank got home as fast as he could and held Marty tight as she cried. Marty thanked Lyn for her help and they took off for the airport.

When she stepped off the plane and saw her brother, he was a lot calmer than she expected. He was in shock. The first thing he wanted to do was ask a check-in clerk at the airport if there was a TV somewhere so they could see the news. Marty told them why and they took Byron and Marty to a private break-room. The scene of the accident was on the news broadcast in full living color. Seeing the car on TV, it was difficult to believe anyone had gotten out alive. They showed a man carrying little Beth's limp body to the ambulance. Byron and Marty felt like they were in a nightmare. They were going to wake up and none of this was actually happening.

When they left the airport, Byron said, "We have to go back to the house before driving on to Great Bend." Marty asked, "So I can help you pack?" He answered in a soft voice, "No, I need you to pick out the clothes for Bernice and Beth to be buried in, I can't do it." Marty took a deep breath and started shaking as she said, "Okay."

They walked into the house and Marty stopped dead in her tracks at the front door. It was so quiet, so empty. Bernice and the kids were not there. Marty felt like someone had just smacked her right across the face! She went upstairs and opened Beth's closet. When she saw all those pretty little dresses, she lost it and had to sit down a few minutes before she could proceed. Then she picked out three of the cutest ones with the tears streaming down her face. She went into Bernice's closet and picked out two of her prettiest dresses. Marty couldn't find a clean bra for Bernice; they were all in the laundry or with her on the trip. Byron said, "Don't worry about it; we'll buy one for her in Great Bend." She took all of the dresses she picked out, and told Byron the mortician could help in the final decision. Ray, the mortician, belonged to the same church as Byron and Bernice when they lived in Great Bend, and they were in the same Bible study together for eight years.

It was past midnight by the time they arrived in Great Bend and went straight to the hospital. There were several nuns in the lobby at the desk. When Byron told them who he was, tears came into their eyes. They knew Alma personally and all about the accident. Bernice's sister, Alma, who was a RN, had worked in that hospital before she moved to Wichita. One of the nuns said, "I'll take you to Brent's room." Marty expected him to be asleep. He was wide awake, just laying there staring at the ceiling like a zombie. Byron and Marty gave him a hug. The room was dark with very little light. The nurse told them before they went in that he was in severe shock. What he saw at the scene of the accident was difficult for an adult to handle, much less a child. So Marty asked Brent softly, "Do you know who I am?" Brent answered, "Sure, you're my aunt in California who has the fish pond. Did you bring Buttons?" (Every year, Marty flew back to Colorado and Kansas to visit family and took Buttons with her. Brent was crazy about Buttons.) She answered softly, "No, I didn't bring him this time honey." He just nodded his head. Brent told Byron later that he knew his mom and sister were dead at the scene of the accident. So Brent didn't even ask Aunt Marty why she was there, he knew. Byron asked the nurse if they could give him something to help him sleep. They left shortly and went to Alma's room but she was asleep. They had her heavily sedated. Byron and Marty left the hospital and went to a coffee shop to eat. They just picked at their food even though neither one of them had eaten since breakfast the day before. Both of them had consumed a ton of coffee.

Then they went over to see Bernice's parents. Her mother, Ruby seemed relieved to see them. Carlos, Bernice's dad, was in bed. They sat around the kitchen table with more coffee for awhile, then she suggested they go lay down for a couple of hours. She told them, "You have a very big day ahead of you." They went to bed, but couldn't sleep. Ruby came into the bedroom where Marty was laying down and said, "I don't want to rush you, but Byron needs to get down to the Mortuary and make all the arrangements." They went down and talked with Ray, the mortician, who was shook up himself since he knew Byron and Bernice so well. They picked out Bernice's casket. They only had one small casket available for Beth. Byron was stoned faced, still in shock. Marty wondered if Byron would even have a memory of this later.

They returned to Ruby's house and Bernice's brother, Loren, had arrived. Byron and Marty still had to buy Bernice's bra and take the clothes down to Ray. Marty asked Loren if he would like to go with them. He said, "Yes, I would." They stopped at a store to buy the bra and Byron had no idea what size Bernice wore. She was a big woman with very large boobs. Loren was a very quiet, shy and reserved guy. Marty picked up a huge bra and asked Byron, "Does this one look about right?" Loren was standing there turning beet red in the face. The poor saleslady did not have a clue what they were doing, or why. She tried to tell Marty what brand would be the best support and Marty was trying to tell her that wasn't important.

Later that afternoon, they went to the florist and picked out long-stemmed red roses for Bernice's casket and miniature pink roses for Beth's casket. Marty thought, "I had no idea when I received roses from Frank for our wedding anniversary four days ago, that I would be standing here today, ordering roses for Bernice and Beth's caskets." Dad and Laura had arrived and went to the florist with them. Laura made a scene telling the florist, "What you are charging is highway robbery! You are taking advantage of people's grief!" Byron and Marty looked at each other, rolling their eyes. Byron motioned for her to step back, away from Laura and Dad. They were too involved trying to run the show to even notice. Byron whispered to Marty, "Thank God we got everything else done before they got here!"

All the rest of the relatives started arriving and they asked Marty if she had her own private jet. They all said, "You came a longer distance than anyone and you were the first one here." They all went to the mortuary together for the viewing. Bernice's wedding rings had slipped around on her finger and Laura reached over to straighten them. Byron said to Marty later, "When Laura fixed Bernice's rings, I could swear I saw Bernice cringe, knowing how Bernice felt about her."

Brent still wasn't talking about the accident. Byron and Marty spent every moment they could with him at the hospital. He just laid there with his face in a comic book for hours. Marty knew Brent wouldn't have realized it, if the book was upside-down. Marty said to Byron, "He needs shock therapy. I think he needs to go down to the mortuary to tell his mama and little sister good-bye. If we don't reach him now, we may never be able to reach him. He has the splint on to hold the leg in place. I think we could do it; we'll just have to be very careful." Byron agreed and told the nurse he needed to talk to Brent's doctor. The minister had already talked to Brent, explaining to him that his mom and little sister went to heaven. He just laid there looking at his comic book not blinking an eye.

The Doctor agreed completely that taking Brent to the mortuary would be good therapy for him, and set everything up with the nurses. He even sent a nurse with them to help maneuver him in and out of the car. Brent had to be carried with his leg in a splint. Byron told Marty and Laura, "You carry him into the chapel. I can't do it." Marty and Laura picked him up together, one on each side, so they could support his leg with the nurse's assistance. They went in, and carried him down to the front of the chapel to see his mom first. He was very quiet, not saying a word. Then they took him over to see his little sister. He looked at her for a long time with a solemn face, but he was swallowing hard. The tears streamed down Marty's face, even the nurse was crying, but not Laura. Marty said to Laura, "Let's sit down for a minute and rest." In a few minutes, they took him up to see them again. Then Marty asked Brent softly, "Do you want to go back to the hospital now?" He just nodded yes. After they returned to the hospital and got him settled back in bed; Marty suggested to Dad and Laura, "Let's all leave the room now, so Byron and Brent can talk." Brent opened up and told Byron all about the accident and exactly how it happened.

Later that evening, Dad and Laura wanted Marty to go over to Helen's with them. Helen was Laura's mother-in-law. Laura's husband and kids were there with other relatives. While they were there, Marty started having severe chest pains and difficulty breathing. Everyone wanted to rush her to the hospital. Marty said, "No way, I'll be fine. I don't have time to lie in a hospital, my brother needs me." Dad asked Helen, "Do you have any fresh lemons?" Helen did and Dad told her to cut one in half. Dad had Marty suck on the fresh lemon and her chest pains calmed down. *It was a remedy from Grandma's old medical book. The book was probably over a hundred years old; the pages were all yellow and falling out of it.*

The service was longer than most funerals because two ministers spoke. The minister in Great Bend had known Bernice and Byron for years, and was the one who married them eleven years ago. In fact, that's how Byron met Bernice, when he started going to church there. The minister in Wichita wanted to speak too and the tears streamed down his face when he talked about little Beth and how her smile always brightened up his day. Bernice was in the church choir and also sung solos for many weddings and funerals. She was also a Sunday school teacher for twenty years, starting when she was just a teenager.

After the service, Marty was in the kitchen helping Ruby, Bernice's mother. Ruby asked Marty, "Don't you think I should have Brent?" Marty stared at her, trying to keep her cool, and said, "Ruby, Byron has lost his entire family except Brent. Brent is all he has in this world now. Brent belongs with his Dad." The next day, Ruby said to Marty, "I sure could use Bernice's refrigerator." Marty asked, "You don't think Byron and Brent will need a frig?"

Byron and Marty checked Brent out of the hospital and took him home in Wichita. Marty got Brent settled in bed upstairs and went downstairs to clean the kitchen. She heard Brent sobbing and ran upstairs. She sat on the bed and held him in her arms when he said, "I can't sleep. Every time I go to sleep, I have all these dreams." Marty asked him, "Do you want to talk about it?" Through his tears, he said, "I can't. I just can't." At that moment, Marty heard Byron downstairs, sobbing like his guts were being torn right out of him. Marty said to Brent, "You lie down, honey, and try to rest. I need to go down to check on your Dad." Brent asked, "Why is Dad crying like that?" Marty replied, "He misses your mom and little sister just like you do, honey." Marty ran downstairs and found Byron on the floor. He had brought Bernice's suitcase in from the car. (The guy at the savage yard had given him all of their things out of the wrecked car.) Byron had laid the suitcase down on the floor, opened it up, and right on top was Beth's doll. Marty was beside herself, trying to comfort both of them. She prayed to God to give them all the strength to get through this. *Marty was a very firm believer that God gives us the strength to get through anything. All we have to do is ask for it. God promised he will never give us a cross we cannot bare.*

Byron received a letter from Laura a couple of days later. She must have mailed it right after they returned to Colorado from the funeral. Laura said, "The accident was God's way of taking you out of an unhappy situation. As far as losing Beth, from a mother's point of view, if something happened to me I wouldn't want to leave my little girl in this world without my protection." Marty was livid! She didn't understand the reason why Laura even wrote the letter. She thought, "If that's how God operated, Estel would have been dead years ago!" It was true that Byron and Bernice's marriage wasn't fantastic, but there is no such thing as a perfect marriage. Marriage is union of two people and no one is perfect.

Byron didn't say much about the letter. He was quiet for a few minutes, and then told Marty, "I have something that is eating on me. It's something I said to Bernice that I have to live with now. Next week, I'm going to be confirmed into the Catholic Church. You know how Bernice felt about the Catholics, being such a strong Baptist. Three days before she died, Brent was baptized into the Baptist Church. We made a deal that if I went to Brent's Baptism, she would go to my confirmation. When we got home from the Baptism, I told her I didn't know how she was going to do it, but I knew she would renege on our deal and not go to my confirmation." Marty just sat there speechless. She had no idea of what to say.

During the day, Marty fixed a bed on the sofa for Brent in the family room so he could watch TV and also eat there. It was difficult for him to sit at the table with his cast. The cast went above his knee, so he couldn't bend his leg. She carried him upstairs every time he had to go to the bathroom. This got old fast, as Brent was no little seven year old. He was quite a chunk to carry up those stairs. Then she started having him pee into a jar. After doing this several times he asked Marty, "Hold it for me." Marty answered, "You're a big boy; you can hold it yourself." His reply was, "I get tired of holding it!" Aunt Marty told him, "Well, you better get used to it, you've got years of *aiming it* ahead of you."

One morning, Marty was trying to cook Byron's breakfast and take care of Brent at the same time. She grabbed the toast out the toaster and tossed it on Byron's plate of bacon and eggs, as she was taking Brent's breakfast to him and set it up on a TV tray. When she returned to the kitchen, Byron was eating dry toast. Marty asked, "Don't you like butter on your toast?" Byron said "yes." She replied, "Then why are you eating it like that?" He answered, "Because you didn't butter for me." A few minutes later, he started looking around the kitchen at the mess Marty made from cooking breakfast and stated, "Boy, Bernice would roll over in her grave if she could see her kitchen now!" Marty just let it pass, and sat down to eat a bite herself. They had been discussing the fact that Bernice's little sister, Carla, had been rude when she came over to do her laundry. She lived in Wichita too and always used Bernice's washer and dryer. Marty suggested, "It must be difficult for Carla to see me here, running her sister's home." Byron said, "Why don't you go to Hays for a week to see Dad. If I can see no difference in her attitude, then we'll know it has nothing to do with you being here and you can come back." Marty took a deep breath and said softly, "Byron, you do know I can't stay here forever. I have Frank and Buttons; my home is in California. If you think you can do without me for a week just to feel out Carla, then I think it's time for me to go home. I haven't said anything to you before, but this Saturday is Bechtel's Christmas party. That's when they always install the new board of directors for BEC each year. It's a social club for the employees. This Saturday, Frank will be installed as the club's treasurer. I would really like to be there for him, if you don't need me anymore here." Byron said, "Oh, of course. I realize you can't stay forever."

Byron talked to his next-door neighbor and she said she would be happy to take care of Brent while Byron was at work. Marty called Dad to ask if he could come down from Hays and stay with Byron for a few days after she left. He said, "No problem. I want to see you again before you leave anyway." He came down and took Marty to the airport. Byron and Brent didn't go, it was too difficult with Brent's leg in a cast. Marty sobbed all the way to the airport, and told her Dad she felt like she was deserting them.

Marty got home the day before the Christmas party. Frank and Buttons were thrilled to have "Mom" home after being gone for three weeks. The next morning, Frank surprised Marty with a beautiful corsage to wear with the evening gown she had bought in San Francisco. Lyn, her friend next door, and Marty were sitting at the table having coffee when Frank walked in and handed Marty the box. Marty opened it and felt the color drain out of her face. She tried not to let on because she didn't want to hurt Frank's feelings. After Frank went outside to work in the yard; Lyn said, "I saw the look on your face. It reminded you of all the flowers at the funeral, didn't it?" Marty answered, "You don't know the half of it. These are exactly the same miniature roses, in the same color, that we ordered for little Beth's casket." Lynn's face went to sheer horror as she said, "Oh my God!"

The Christmas party that night was in the Grand Ballroom at the Marriott Hotel with over a thousand people attending. It was beautiful, with live music and dancing. They sat at the head table with all the other board members. Marty wasn't in a festive mood, but she was happy to be there to see Frank installed as the BEC Treasurer.

During the next five months, Marty called Byron every week to give him support. He wanted to get out of Wichita, away from all the memories. Marty asked if he would be interested in moving to California. When Brent's school let out for the summer; Byron quit his job, rented out his house, packed up the car, and drove to California.

They lived with Frank and Marty for two months. Marty could not get Byron to look for a job. He just sat around all day doing absolutely nothing. Brent was okay except he was in a shell. There was a boy next door his age and they became best friends. Both of the boys loved Buttons, and the three of them had a good time in the back yard.

Byron talked about getting a job and finding an apartment. At first, he wanted Marty to take care of Brent while he was working, and she told him, "No problem, I would be happy to." Then he decided he wanted to just leave Brent there, to live with them. He started laying out the ground rules. Frank and Marty were expected to take Brent everywhere they went socially. He said, "Bernice and I didn't believe in baby sitters." Marty told him, "You are expecting us to take Brent everywhere with us. We wouldn't have done that with our own children if we had them. You are asking me to make Brent the center of my whole world! What happens to me when you get married again; you will want your son with you and rightfully so. I'm not going to set myself up for that." Byron exploded, "This is not you talking, its Frank! He's the one against this! You are putting your husband first instead of me. I'm your blood!" By now Byron is screaming at the top of his lungs. Marty yelled back, "You damn well better

believe Frank is first, because that's the way it's supposed to be!"
Byron packed all of their things and left. He wouldn't tell Marty
where they were going or what he was going to do. They went to
Great Bend, back to Kansas. He left Brent with his mother-in-
law, Ruby, for two years until he was settled in a permanent job
again and ready to provide a home for Brent.

CHAPTER TWENTY-NINE

A letter came from Vernon—he was coming home from Vietnam! Marty was so excited and relieved, she counted the days! Vernon said he would call them from LAX when he arrived because he didn't know the flight number or time, only what airline and date. Marty told Frank, "There's no way I want him to step off that plane with no one there to welcome him home!" Marty called reservations for the airline and explained the situation to the operator; then told her, "I think he's flying into Japan with a layover in Hawaii." The operator said, "Let me check." A couple of minutes later, she came back on the phone and told Marty the flight number and time of arrival in LAX.

When Vernon stepped off that plane and saw his Aunt Marty and Uncle Frank standing there waiting to greet him, the look on his face was priceless! Aunt Marty was crying, but this time they were tears of joy! They took him to the restaurant at the top of the tower in LAX, with a beautiful view of the city lights, but Vernon was very quiet. As if coming home from Nam wasn't enough to deal with, he was thinking about how he was going to handle the situation he was coming home to with Joann. He found out from his friends in Kansas that Joann was screwing around with other guys—even Vernon's little brother, Tom. Tom grew up to be a mess, putting it mildly. Frank and Marty already knew all about it. Vernon and Marty wrote to each other every week during his tour duty in Vietnam.

Vernon was going to be saying "hi" and "good-by" to his son he hadn't seen in eighteen months! Buddy wasn't even going to know his Daddy. Vernon was a very tender hearted guy and he loved his boy dearly. He was going to fly into Wichita, Kansas and take a bus home to Hutchinson. No one knew he was coming, not even his parents. Vernon had told no one but Frank and Marty that he was coming home. He wanted to "catch" Joann off guard—with her pants down, literally.

Frank and Marty took Vernon home with them for a couple of days before he flew out to Kansas. Marty talked Vernon into calling his dad the next day. She told him, "Just tell him not to tell your wife or anyone else you are coming home and why. You can trust your dad." She knew he certainly couldn't trust his mom, Marty's sister. His dad was thrilled when he heard Vernon's voice! He asked, "Where are you?" Vernon told him, "I'm at Marty and Frank's house in California." He promised not to tell anyone and said, "I'll pick you up at the airport in Wichita!" Sure enough, Vernon caught Joann red-handed himself and filed for divorce. It sure wasn't any kind of homecoming for a soldier who's been off to war for eighteen months! There were no yellow ribbons around the old oak tree for Vernon.

CHAPTER THIRTY

Out of the blue, Marty's Dad called one day. He said, "You're not going to believe this, but I stopped by to see your Mom Phillips and took her out to dinner. I have feelings toward her now that I didn't know were still in me. I thought I was too old to fall in love again. Marty was shocked out of her mind, but she was happy for him.

Marty dated Mildred's son, Bob, during their senior year in high school. Mildred became her mom and remained to be her mom after Bob and Marty broke up. After all these years, she still went to see Mildred every year when she went to Kansas to visit family.

A few months later, Marty started having pains in her abdomen. They did an exploratory surgery and found an infection. The doctor thought it would clear up, but it kept getting worse. It got to the point it was too painful to have sex. She increased her pain medication just to get through the day. Marty had been on pain medication since their car accident three years ago. Frank recovered very well from his fractured back, but Marty had permanent damage in her neck and left shoulder from the severe whiplash in addition to the problems she had in her back from her childhood.

Dad and Mildred flew out to California one week after her exploratory surgery. Frank was taking two weeks of vacation from work and they were remodeling the kitchen, tearing everything out down to the bare walls. A cabinet company was building and installing the cabinets plus the countertops. Dad and Frank installed everything else; new appliances, sink, and lighting. It wasn't until after they had the kitchen completely torn out that Dad told Marty he was having surgery in December. He had a double hernia plus a tendon causing problems in his hand. He was going to have it all taken care of in Colorado, where Laura lived, after the kitchen was completed. Marty wanted to hit him and asked, "Why didn't you tell me this before we planned this kitchen? You have no business doing all this lifting with a double hernia!" He insisted that he would be just fine as long as he had on his hernia belt.

Marty almost had a nervous breakdown through it all and she was in a lot of pain herself. When Mildred told her she was coming with Dad, Marty asked her to wait and come next year, because they wouldn't have the time to entertain her and take her places. Marty explained that they would be working on the kitchen and not have time for fun. Mildred said, "No, I want to come now. Don't you worry about entertaining me; all I care about is spending time with you and your daddy." Two days after they arrived, Mildred started complaining, "Aren't we going anywhere or do anything?" Marty wanted to scream! They had fruit and cold breakfast cereal in the morning, sandwiches for lunch, and went out every night for dinner. They had to move the old refrigerator into the garage so Marty made many trips back and forth to serve breakfast and lunch. Then she washed the dishes in the garage sink. It was certainly not a time to have a demanding house guest who was constantly complaining!

When Dad and Mildred arrived, Marty put their luggage in separate bedrooms. After they were there a few days, Marty said to her dad when no one else was around, "I don't care where you sleep Dad, you are a big boy. But if you are not going to sleep in your own bed, please don't mess it up so it looks like you've slept in it. I really don't enjoy making beds that much." He blushed and was so embarrassed, he left the room! But Marty didn't have to continue making three beds everyday.

They were taking the day off and going to Disneyland so Mildred would feel she did something on her vacation to California. Frank went back to work after taking two weeks off. The kitchen was back to being a functional kitchen again, close to completion. Before they left that morning, Dad and Marty were standing in the kitchen talking. Marty asked Dad, "What is that dripping I hear?" He answered, "I don't hear anything," and went on talking. Marty broke in, "I hear water dripping!" She stood there looking up at the ceiling, trying to think what it could be when she saw water dripping into the light fixture! Dad immediately crawled up into the attic and found the attic flooded above the kitchen! He had the water line to the refrigerator for the ice maker disconnected for nearly two weeks while everything was torn up in the kitchen. When Dad installed the ice maker in the new frig, the copper water line above the kitchen in the attic and down the inside of the wall, sprung leaks caused by alkali! After turning off the water to the copper line, they poked holes in the kitchen ceiling to let it drain—into buckets, pans and anything else they could find to catch the water. They saved the new kitchen! Dad said, "If we had gone to Disneyland before discovering it, the ceiling would have fallen before we got home." They still went to Disneyland that day and rented a wheelchair for Mildred because she couldn't walk that much. The next day, they put a fan in the attic to dry it out completely. Several days later, Dad replaced the water line and repaired the ceiling.

When her dream kitchen was completed, the first meal Marty prepared was tossed salad; spaghetti with meatballs; and garlic bread. They had a bottle of cold duck to celebrate their new kitchen. When Frank popped the cork, it sprayed the entire kitchen: ceiling, floor, new appliances, and all over the beautiful new cabinets! Marty just stood there, cracking up. Frank looked at her like she had lost her mind and said, "How can you stand there laughing after all this work and now it's a mess?" Marty replied, "It's better to laugh than cry!" She was up all night cleaning. Everything had to be washed and polished from top to bottom. When she finished, it all looked beautiful once again.

Mildred had to leave before Dad. She was still working and had to get back to the office. The night before she left, they went to a Hawaiian restaurant. Dad went wild over the hula girls, acting like a teenage boy turned loose in a whore house! He was really being an ass, but Marty was so fed up with Mildred she didn't care. You could almost see the steam coming out of Mildred's ears!

When they got home that night, Marty and Mildred got into it, big time! She saw a side of Mildred she had not seen before now. She had no consideration or appreciation of the mess they were in while remodeling the kitchen. The next day, when they put Mildred on the plane to go home, Marty was so pissed she didn't even say good-bye. It was several months before Marty made up with Mildred. After they made up, Mildred told Marty's dad, "I feel like I have my daughter back."

Dad left a couple of weeks after Mildred and flew into Denver. He had his surgeries and everything went very well. He stayed at Laura's for several weeks until he was able to work again. Frank and Marty paid his medical bills that his insurance didn't cover.

CHAPTER THIRTY-ONE

Two months later, Marty was still living with a lot of pain. One day the pain was so bad that she called the doctor's office and told them she needed to come in that day. Dr. Jackson had the day off and she saw the gynecologist who was on call. The doctor walked into the room with her chart in his hand and said, "It says here that Dr. Jackson suspects that you have a tubular pregnancy." Marty started laughing. The doctor gave her a strange look and asked, "What's funny about a tubular pregnancy? That's very painful!" Marty replied, "Because my husband is sterile and Dr. Jackson knows that! I thought Dr. Jackson was acting like he wanted to ask me something, but didn't have the nerve. Now I know what it was; he wanted to know if I've been cheating on my husband. I assure you, I have not!" Marty went home and called Lyn next door. Lyn said, "It's time you changed doctors." Lyn gave Marty the name and phone number of another gynecologist and they got her in the next day. Four days later, Marty had a complete hysterectomy. She was so full of endometriosis, her new doctor didn't know how she stood the pain.

Marty was just released from the hospital when her grandmother passed away and Frank's mom was having a lot of pain in her stomach and back. Mom took a few days off work, but didn't improve, so she went to her doctor and was hospitalized for tests. Mom had advanced stages of cancer. The doctor said she would not last six months. Dad insisted that the doctor or no one else could tell Mom. They were all expected to put up a false front to Mom that she was going to get well just by taking her pills. The pills were actually for her pain.

Right after they received the results of the tests, Marty and Frank went over to pick up Dad and took him to the hospital. It was so difficult to see Mom and not let on that they had received the horrible news of her cancer. When they took Dad home he said, "I need your help to take your mother's things to the garage. I want them out of here!" They didn't know what to say or do but oblige and helped him carry her things to the garage.

A couple of days later, Marty went to the hospital with Dad in the afternoon. They talked to the doctor in the hall and he said he would be sending Mom home in a couple of days. Dad started screaming at the doctor, "You can't do that to me! What am I supposed to do with her? I can't take care of her! Put her in a home or something!" The doctor was very firm with Dad and said, "She needs to be home! She deserves to be at home! I can give you phone numbers to hire someone to come in daily to help." Dad went into a total panic! He asked Marty to help put back all of Mom's things the way she had them. He said, "She would kill me if she knew what I did with her things!" As usual, the bastard was only thinking of himself.

Marty was going through the surgical change of life brought on by her hysterectomy. They had to remove all of her female organs including both ovaries. She was going crazy with hot flashes and coming unglued over little things, much less the fact she was losing her mother-in-law who she adored! Dick, Frank's brother-in-law, informed Marty that her change of life was all in her head. Marge and Dick never showed an ounce of concern or understanding for anything Marty and Frank went through, but let *them* have something and the whole damn world was supposed to come to attention!

When Marge was in high school, she had cancer and they removed half of her stomach. She recovered very well, but had to have physicals religiously. Four months before Marty's hysterectomy, they removed a small tumor from Marge's stomach. Marty was standing right there when the doctor said it was benign, but Marge told everyone she had cancer again. Three months later, Marge had lung surgery. The doctors had found a spot on her lungs and told her she could have surgery or they could keep an eye on it. Marge opted for the surgery. It was just a spot from an old infection. She went through all that pain for nothing!

Dad hired a nurse to come in every morning to bath Mom and do whatever she needed. Marty and Marge were alternating days to go over to Mom and Dad's, but Marge said she couldn't do any cleaning because of her surgery two months ago. Marty had surgery two weeks ago, but helped anyway. It never occurred to her that Dad could well afford to hire a cleaning lady. Once again, Marty was a complete idiot!

It was important for Frank to come home from work, remove his shoe and sock, and elevate his bad foot in the recliner. Three times a week, Marty spent the day with Mom and Dad while she did their laundry, cleaned, fixed lunch and then prepared dinner. Frank came over directly from work. After dinner, Frank and Marty did the dishes and cleaned up the kitchen. They talked for a while and then Marty helped Mom get ready for bed before they left. After doing this routine for a couple of weeks, Frank came home from work one day with his bad foot swollen beyond belief! Marty called his doctor immediately and he asked her to bring Frank to his office as fast as she could get him there. Frank had blood poisoning in his foot. Dr. Bleecker gave him a shot and told Frank he was going into the hospital. Frank answered, "No way!" Dr. Bleecker replied, "Then you are going to use crutches and stay off your foot completely for one week. No work!" He gave Frank a prescription and wanted to see him the next day. Dr. Bleecker was Frank's doctor when he was in the car accident in 1960. He was personally protective of Frank's leg and foot, being so proud of the fact he had saved them from amputation in addition to saving Frank's life!

Frank and Marty stopped by Mom and Dad's after leaving the doctor's office because they were in the vicinity. They came unglued when they saw Frank on crutches. Marty explained to them what happened, but didn't say a word about what brought it on, not wanting them to feel guilty. They reassured Mom and Dad that he would be just fine, but he had to be on crutches for a week. After they got home, Marge and Dick called, ripping Frank and Marty up one side and down the other for upsetting the folks! *No concern for Frank and the fact he could have lost his leg or died! As usual, it happened to Frank and Marty so it was no big deal!*

Marty went in for her check up from her hysterectomy. Her doctor was upset because she wasn't healing well and was passing blood. He accused her of having sex when he had told her, no sex for at least six weeks. She told him, "I have not had sex! I don't have time for sex! My mother-in-law has terminal cancer. I'm going over there to do their laundry, cooking, and cleaning in addition to my own." The doctor replied, "I'm sorry to hear that, but isn't there someone else who can help? You are in no condition to do all that at home yet, much less for your in-laws." Marty said, "There is no one else. My sister-in-law had lung surgery two months ago. My husband is on crutches now because of blood poisoning in his bad foot." The doctor looked at her in disbelief and said, "Oh is that all?" Marty answered, "No, my Grandmother died last month and my Dad had surgery in December." The doctor held up both hands and said, "Stop! Stop! You are going to have me in tears! I can't believe what you are dealing with while you are going through the surgical change of life! The surgical change of life is much more difficult than the natural way because your body goes into it abruptly and not gradually. If you could hear the small and petty complaints I hear from my other patients who are going through the change of life! I can't believe everything you are dealing with and not complaining!" Marty just said, "Doc, you do what you have to do." She's thinking to herself though, "You don't know the half of it. You don't know what assholes we are dealing with on top of everything else." Marty never said a word to Mom or Dad that she wasn't healing properly, but she started cooling it and wasn't so ambitious now. She told Marge, but might as well of told it to the wind. Marge made no comment and showed no concern whatsoever!

A few months later, it became obvious to Mom that she wasn't going to get better. On the days Marty went over there, Frank removed his shoe and sock on his bad foot and elevated it there during the evening, so the blood poisoning would not return. One night when Marty was helping Mom get ready for bed, Mom started crying and told Marty she wasn't ready to die. Marty held her and cried with her. She said, "Mom, I love you so much, I don't want you to go either. I would give anything in the world if I could take your pain away." A month later, Mom was gone.

When they went to the mortuary to make the arrangements, there was no reverence to Dad's mannerism. He walked into the room and announced, "I want to tell you before we even begin; I want the cheapest damn funeral you've got!" When the mortuary called to say they were ready for the viewing, Dad didn't even want to go. He was upset with Marge because she wanted to go see Mom. He said to Frank and Marty, "If she goes, I have to go." Marty told him, "I want to go too, so you can be mad at both of us." So they all went to the mortuary for the viewing. Dad stood there looking at Mom and said flatly, "good-bye Ann". After Frank and Marty took him home, he said he was glad he went, that it helped to say good-bye. They stayed with Dad for a week after Mom died. The next door neighbor took care of Buttons for them. She helped a lot with Buttons during the seven months Mom was sick.

Frank and Marty went through a really tough time of it. Both of them were trying to deal with their grief in their own way. Instead of it bringing them closer together, they were growing a part. Marty was still going over to Dad's three times a week; keeping him company, doing his laundry, cooking and cleaning. It still never occurred to her that he could well afford to hire a cleaning lady. What an idiot!

Three months after Mom was gone, Dad announced to Frank and Marty one evening, "I'm going to take you both to Las Vegas as a thank you for helping me through this thing. Marty, you set it up and we'll go." The three of them went in Dad's car and after they arrived, Dad's attitude toward Marty changed immediately. During Mom's illness and after she was gone, Marty was the greatest thing on two legs because she was there for him. Now, that he was in Vegas and had his son; he acted like he would have loved it if Marty would disappear into the woodwork. They got tickets to see the Dean Martin show. Marty said, "We have to get in line early for the show to get good seats." (This was before they had assigned seating in the showrooms.) Dad said to Frank in her presence, "Let her stand in line, let's go gamble, to hell with her!" Marty stood in line for nearly one hour. Standing in one spot was difficult for her with her back. She first started to feel dizzy and then she thought she was going to pass out. The line finally started moving, but when she got to the door of the showroom, Dad and Frank were no where in sight. She had to step aside and let people go ahead of her. They finally came and Dad wouldn't let Marty tip the maitre d' five dollars in order to get good seats. He shoved her hand that held out the five dollar bill back to her chest and yelled at her right in front of the maitre d', "That's a total waste of money!" The maitre d' seated them as far back as he possibly could, against the back wall and it was a very large showroom. It could have been Peter Pan on the stage instead of Dean Martin and you wouldn't know the difference! Marty stood in line all that time for absolutely nothing! She was so pissed that she wanted to walk out of there, take a taxi to the airport and fly home without even telling them, but she knew if she did there would be hell to pay.

Marty did not go over to Dad's again to cook or clean; he was on his own except for help from his precious little Marge. Frank and Marty were growing a part more and more. The winter that year was colder than normal and Marty got a severe case of bursitis in her bad shoulder from their car accident. She couldn't even dress herself and started thinking about their life in general. All they did was slave on the damn house. She said to Frank one day, "Let's go look at townhouses." Frank looked at her in shock and asked, "Where did this come from?" Marty answered, "I can't work in the yard like I used to and you can't do it all. I think we should be in a townhouse." Frank was thrilled that she finally saw the light! After listing the house with a realtor, it was sold on the first day of open house! The realtor said, "I didn't have to do a thing, your show place sold itself! The house almost doubled in price during the seven years they owned it. Real estate had gone up, plus they had made many improvements on the place inside and out.

Two weeks later, they bought a new townhouse in Placentia, so Frank would be closer to work. Frank's Dad was furious because they would be forty miles away. The distance Frank had to drive to work everyday was less important than being closer to him. He brought it up again and again until Marty said to him, "How can you bitch about forty lousy miles? My Dad is fourteen hundred miles away!" He never brought it up again.

It was a lovely complex, only four units in each building and the buildings were all one story. Their unit had an atrium and Marty hired a professional landscaper to build a large waterfall that had nine spillways with a small pond, surrounded by tropical plants. You had a view of it from the kitchen, living room and sitting room.

Two weeks after moving in, Marty joined the Newcomers Club. The club covered the area of three cities; Placentia, Yorba Linda, and Anaheim Hills. She joined several activities in the club, including bridge groups for ladies and couples. (Frank and Marty had learned how to play bridge when they were newlyweds.) Frank was still on the BEC Board of Directors at Bechtel Engineering. He ran for BEC President that year and won. They were on a social whirlwind! Life was great again!

CHAPTER THIRTY-TWO

One evening, Marty walked in from attending a Newcomers board meeting and Frank was on the phone with Laura, Marty's sister. He had a very strange look on his face. Laura's oldest son, Ray, was killed in a car accident on the way home for work. He was only twenty-one years old.

Marty was devastated! She had always been very close to Ray. Marty kept saying, "Not Ray, not my boy!" Ray looked like Laura. He was special, a very tender hearted guy. His younger brother, Roy was always such a smart ass growing up and took after his Dad. Marty called the airlines and packed her bags in record time. Frank took her to the airport that night and she flew into Denver.

The circumstances of the accident were revealed. Ray had installed a high-performance engine in his car and got in a hassle with the cops all the time. He started taking a two-way road to and from work instead of going on the highway to avoid the police. On the night of the accident, a policeman saw him on this country road and was pursuing him. If he got one more ticket, he would lose his license. He also had paraphernalia in the trunk of his car for smoking pot. Ray was speeding around a curve when an elderly lady was turning into her driveway right in front of him. He took the ditch to avoid hitting her and rolled his car. The Boulder Newspaper had it on the front page the next day. The headline read, "Police chase ends in death." They made it sound like he was a common criminal. Laura blamed the police for her son's death. It wasn't the high-performance engine or Ray's reckless driving, it was the "pigs". Marty asked her not to use the word "pig", but she couldn't reason with her.

Roy told Marty, "Mom found out we were smoking pot and started growing it for us. She didn't want us spending all that money on it. Don't tell Mom I told you this, she would kill me." Later, Laura told Marty that she was going to let Roy take the high-performance engine out of Ray's wrecked car and put it in his car. *Marty nearly had a stroke! What was Laura thinking!*

While Marty was gone to Colorado for the funeral, Buttons entertained himself. Marty had a candy dish on an end table in the living room full of wrapped candy. One day while Frank was at work, Buttons took all of the wrapped candy and lined them up all in a row in the back of the sofa seat. The wrappers were still in tact, he was just trying to hide them for a rainy day. When Frank came home, he could barely see the wrappers sticking out from the cushions. Buttons came unglued when Daddy threw out his treasured candy.

Buttons always liked his stash. One time in the Glendora house, Marty discovered a small pile of doggie treats behind the TV. Buttons got one every time he went out to go potty. One day, he got the bright idea of going out more often, to get more treats. Marty had trained him to "go" in the side yard by the garage, not in the yards in front or back of the house. She noticed he was going out a lot, and quietly walked out to peek around the corner of the house to see what he was doing. He went around the corner just far enough so she couldn't see him. After standing there for a couple of minutes doing nothing, he turned around to come back in for his treat. He jumped two feet when he turned around and saw Mom standing there, watching him.

They were always cracking up at something Buttons did, he was their little clown. When Buttons was mad at Mom for going next door to have coffee with Lyn, he would go into the master bath and tee-pee the whole bathroom. One time, Mom caught him in the act. He stood on his hind legs and spun the toilet tissue roll around by batting at it with his front paws as fast as he could, unrolling the whole roll. Then he pulled it with his teeth and strung it all over the bathroom.

One year when they got home from the Bechtel Christmas party, they found half of the Christmas gifts under the tree unwrapped. Buttons got bored and thought, "Why should I wait until Christmas to get all my goodies?" Every year, Santa brought Buttons a new sweater, collar and leash, plus he got a lot of different doggie treats. He tore open the gifts until he got to his and had a jolly good time eating all of his snacks.

The following summer, after Ray's death, Frank and Marty flew to Colorado on vacation. Dad, Byron and Brent were there too for a family get together at Laura's. Frank and Marty took Buttons with them and he was in his carrier in the baggage department. When their plane landed in Denver, the captain announced over the intercom, "Mrs. Wurtz, report to the check-in counter of gate twenty-one." Marty freaked out and said to Frank, "Something is wrong with Buttons!" Frank told her to calm down, that he was sure everything was fine. She ran off the plane and said to Dad and Laura, who were standing there waiting to greet them, "Something's wrong with Buttons!" She charged over to the counter, but the attendant wouldn't tell her anything. Instead, she said curtly, "Just follow me please." Marty followed the lady out the door and down the stairs outside, with Laura right behind her. Several guys were standing there by the plane and one of them was holding Buttons; he looked like he was way out there in twilight zone by the look in his eyes. He had clawed and chewed his way out of his carrier. Then he found the outside door of the plane in the baggage compartment and clawed off the insulation on the door down to the bare steel as far up as he could reach. Marty took Buttons and thought he would be okay. She then noticed all the insulation on the ground. Laura saw it too and asked, "What's all that stuff on the ground?" One of the guys answered, "That's what your dog did lady!" Marty looked up and saw the number her little darling had done to the airplane door and asked, "What do we do about that?" As she was thinking, "Oh boy, this is going to be two grand or more to fix their door." They replied, "Don't worry about it; our insurance will take care of it." Laura and Marty took Buttons up the stairs to where they had left Frank and Dad. Frank asked, "What happened?" Marty replied, "Your son got bored and tried to destroy that 747."

The next day, they all went camping in the Colorado Mountains by a beautiful lake. Buttons was in his glory walking around, enjoying nature with his Daddy. All Laura and Marty did was work; cooking and cleaning up. Everything had to be made from scratch to meet Laura's standards. God forbid if they used bisquit to make pancakes! Laura and Marty had completely different ideas about life. It was almost as if they lived on different planets.

When they returned from their camping trip, Marty called and begged the airlines to let her buy a regular ticket for Buttons to take him aboard in a new carrier and strap it in a seat. They wouldn't allow it and he was too big to fit under the seat in a carrier. They insisted that there was no way he could get out of their carrier, so Marty bought a new one from them. She wasn't going to give Buttons a tranquilizer because she thought that was the problem. In the past, she used mild tranquilizers from the pet store. This time she got them from the Vet. The airline check-in clerk talked her into giving him one. She had given him two for the flight into Denver.

After they arrived at the Ontario airport in California, they were outside waiting to pick up Buttons and their luggage when they saw the luggage tractor drive up. Buttons was sitting on top of the luggage with his big floppy ears flapping in the breeze! He could have fallen off or jumped off the tractor! He had gotten out of their carrier, spreading the steel bars apart like an ape in a horror movie! Marty rescued him and thought he would be okay. Frank took Buttons to their neighbor who was picking them up and came back to help Marty with their luggage. They got the suitcases but were still waiting for their clothes bags after the guys had unloaded everything. Marty said to one of them, "We are still waiting for our clothes bags." He brought them out. This time, instead of attacking the airplane, Buttons found their clothes bags and destroyed them. The clothes were fine, but the bags were completely shredded. The guy started apologizing, "I'm really sorry, but we had a problem.

We had Jaws aboard!" Marty told him, "Don't worry about it, Jaws belongs to us."

Buttons didn't touch anyone else's bags, just Frank and Marty's. The next morning, Marty took Buttons in to see the Vet. He checked Buttons out and said he would be fine. He also verified what Marty thought, the problem was the tranquilizers. He said, "Never give Buttons tranquilizers again; they caused him to go on a bad trip just like he was on PCP. It was a miracle that he lived through it once, much less twice!" Marty answered, "He will never get another tranquilizer. There won't even be a reason to because he will never fly again."

CHAPTER THIRTY-THREE

Frank and Marty continued on their social whirlwind, having the time of their lives! Between BEC and Newcomers Club, they were on the go constantly every week-end. Marty was chairman of three bridge groups and the Gad Abouts. She was also on the committee for Couples Night Out. As BEC President, Frank organized over a hundred social events for the year. They went to: Disneyland in Anaheim, the J. Paul Getty Museum in Malibu, Santa Anita Racetrack in Arcadia, Hollywood Bowl for the Olivia Newton-John concert, the Ice Capades in the L.A. Forum, Ramona Pageant in Hemet, a rodeo in the L.A. Forum, a luau at the Disneyland Hotel, the summer dinner dance and cruise at the Balboa Pavilion, and cruised to Catalina Island on a yacht, to name just a few.

The Couples Night Out in the Newcomers Club had a party once a month. One month they had a luau and after a few drinks, no one was feeling any pain. Some of the guys started throwing people into the swimming pool. Frank and Marty were thrown in too, fully dressed. Since their clothes were wet anyway, they just sat on the steps of the pool in the water. Frank told Marty, "It's time for us to go home, Babe; things are getting out of hand." Marty replied, "Don't be such a party pooper! I'm having fun!" Then all of a sudden, she saw a pair of panties floating in the pool! She looked around and saw a few of the girls in the pool were topless! One of the topless gals was the hostess. Her husband yelled at her, "Go up to your room, now!" Marty said to Frank, "Oh my! I think you're right. It really is time to go home!" They left by the side gate so they wouldn't drip water on the carpet going through the house. When they got into the car, Marty was so cold with her long wet dress on, she took it off. They prayed all the way home that a cop wouldn't pull them over with her sitting there in her wet panties and bra.

Marty was voted the most valuable member of the Newcomers Club for the year and elected First Vice-President and Editor of the monthly Newsletter for the following year.

Frank and Marty went to Las Vegas with three other couples for the weekend. After seeing the Mac Davis show, they all went over to the Aladdin Casino. Marty played blackjack for awhile and started to leave the table when she saw a man fall on the floor about ten feet away. Security guards seemed to come out of the woodwork. They came from every direction. The man had been fatally shot with a silencer. Marty saw Ina and Frank right away. She said to Frank, "Round everyone up and let's get out of here. Ina and I will meet you all at the side door." While Ina and Marty were waiting, the paramedics brought out the corpse right in front of them, covered with a sheet. It really let the air out of everyone and they were thankful it was their last night there. Marty told Frank she didn't care if she ever came back to Vegas again.

A few months later, Frank and Marty took a Caribbean Cruise with Frank's boss and his wife, who were close friends. The food, activities, entertainment and the shopping were incredible! *On the ship, they assigned everyone to a table in the dining room, to dine with the same people every meal of the entire Cruise.* The two couples had been assigned to sit at a table with some real drips. On the second day, they managed to get reassigned to a different table and they had a great time. The table on the first night had a mother and daughter. The daughter's hair was not styled, she wore no make up and was modestly dressed. Later that night, Frank and Marty went up to the late night lounge with their friends, where they had a live band and dancing. They all did a double take! There sitting at the bar, surrounded by guys, was Miss Plain herself! She had been very busy after her mama retired for the night. She fixed her hair, put on a lot of make up, and was wearing a short, sexy red dress. Sitting on a bar stool, she had her legs hiked up so the guys could see she wasn't wearing panties. The next morning, Miss Plain was back with Mama in her *drab look*. This was her routine for the entire cruise! Whatever floats your boat!

The Couples Duplicate Bridge group decided to go to Palm Springs for the weekend and stayed at the Tennis Club Hotel. Saturday night, they went to a lovely restaurant that had a piano bar. One of the guys had the piano player make an announcement on the microphone, "Dr. Al Vasher is needed in the men's room for an emergency vasectomy!" Then the piano player sang, "Tip Toe through the Tulips." John, the attorney in the group, stood on the seat of his chair and danced like a fairy tip toeing. He was usually a very straight-laced guy, but he wasn't feeling any pain. Shortly after that, a guy across the room asked them where they were from and John said, "Placentia and Yorba Linda." The guy came up to John and said, "I'm from Placentia, what street do you live on?" John answered, "We're on Six Nations." The guy said, "I live on your street! Wait a minute, I know you, you just bought a new Cadillac this week." John didn't believe him. He thought someone in their group set the whole thing up, like the joke on Al, until the guy said, "You know who I am! I'm the one with the freaking dogs that crap on your lawn all the time!" John sobered up fast! He said to his wife, Kathy, "We have to go home and put the house up for sale. There's no way we can stay in that neighborhood now!"

Marty stayed on course with their social whirlwind until the spring of 1978. She was having problems with her stomach, losing weight and in general, looking pretty bad. She was tired and depressed all the time. It got to the point she would start crying and not be able to stop. She couldn't even tell Frank why she was crying—she didn't know. Marty went to see a phychiatrist and he admitted her into the hospital. In her therapy sessions with Dr. Boyer he asked her over and over, "Do you know how angry you are?" She didn't know what he was talking about, but he continued to hammer away on it. When he finally got her to face all the resentment she had toward her father, the anger just poured out of her, like a broken dam. He put her on 300 mg of Elavil as a mood elevator and to help her sleep. Her stomach problems were getting worse, but Dr. Boyer still blamed it on her emotional state of mind.

When Marty's weight dropped to ninety-three pounds and she was vomiting a lot, Dr. Boyer decided it was more than depression and referred her to a M.D. he knew personally. They put her through several tests at the hospital. The doctor told her, "Go home for the weekend and come back to the hospital Monday morning. Call me if you have any problems." The next morning, Marty had the dry heaves and was in bad shape. Frank called the doctor and said, "She is not going to make it through the week-end!" His reply was, "I didn't think she would, take her to the hospital." Frank got her there, but her veins had collapsed from her being acutely dehydrated. It seemed to take forever and fifty stabs later, for them to get the IV needle into a vein. All the nurses kept apologizing to her, "I'm so sorry, but we have to do this." They fed her through the IV for several days to build her up for surgery. Marty prayed to God that if this was her time, she was ready to go. She told her Dad on the phone, "I've never felt closer to my maker than I do now." He was on the first plane to California. Marty had her surgery and she almost died on the table. After she was back in her room, the nurses wouldn't give her anything for the pain. Frank begged them to give her something, but they couldn't because her blood pressure was dangerously low.

They found a blockage in the opening of her stomach going to the intestine. They identified the blockage as an extra pancreas. Marty asked the doctor, "Do I still have a pancreas?" He replied, "That's the first thing I checked. Yes, you do." She bounced back very fast and she was dismissed a week after the surgery.

Frank and Dad brought Marty home from the hospital in the evening and they stopped at a coffee shop to eat on the way home. When they got home, Frank took Buttons outside to potty after he smothered Mom with his kisses. Marty had not even sat down when Dad asked her, "What's to eat?" *They had dinner just twenty minutes ago at the coffee shop!* Marty bit her lip and said, "I have no idea; I haven't been around here for a while." She looked and said, "There's ice cream." Dad said, "That sounds good, I'll have some of that." Then he sat down at the table to be served. One week ago, they didn't know if she was going to live or die. Now that she was home, she was expected to *immediately* be her father's maid again! Marty took the ice cream, a bowl with a spoon and slammed them down on the table and said, "Here, dish it out yourself! I just damn near died, had major surgery, and I'm still recuperating! Dad looked at her like she had slapped him across the face! She didn't care; he asked for it. It didn't change a damn thing! He still expected her to wait on him like she had all of her life! *At home, he took care of himself, but put him under the same roof with one of his daughters and he became instantly helpless!*

Two days later, when Dad got out of bed to be served breakfast; Marty had a news flash for him. "I have booked you on a flight back home tonight. Frank will take you to the airport when he gets home from work. I know when you came out here, you left in the middle of a job and you need to get back to it. The crisis is over now, I'm going to live." Dad just looked at her and didn't say a word. She helped him pack his bags and he was gone that night.

It was two and a half years before Marty sent her Dad another plane ticket to come out for a visit. Normally, she sent him a plane ticket every year. She also told Frank, "I'm not going back to Kansas or Colorado to visit family ever again! I have had it!" *The last trip was when Buttons let the airlines know what he thought of their accommodations.*

CHAPTER THIRTY-FOUR

After being in the Newcomers Club for three years, Marty and her bridge friends decided to drop out and form their own bridge groups. Marty put together three groups: couples party bridge, ladies daytime duplicate bridge, and ladies daytime party bridge. They already had a duplicate bridge group for couples that another gal had put together. Marty was still considered the bridge chairman. She took care of all the problems, the duplicate score sheets, and made out the hostess schedules.

Marty's Dad and Mildred were still very close. Mildred's son Bob and his family were living on Oahu. Frank and Marty flew over to Hawaii and stayed in the Waikiki Outrigger Hotel on the beach. Their suite had a great view of the ocean and Diamond Head from their lanai. Bob and his wife, Theresa, took them to a lovely restaurant with an incredible view, and also took them snorkeling the next day. The snorkeling was great—after Marty swallowed half the ocean getting the hang of it. They all had a fabulous time! The rest of the time, Frank and Marty did some shopping, sunbathed on the beach, saw Pearl Harbor, plus the cultural center. On the last night, they went to the Germaine's Luau; that was truly authentic, out in the middle of nowhere on a beach.

The next day, Frank and Marty flew over to Maui and stayed in a condo on the beach. It had a breathtaking view from their lanai too! The first night, they had dinner in a restaurant that was magnificent. There was a small brook running through the restaurant with the outside wall next to the beach completely open. Beautiful little birds were flying around and Marty wondered if they were housebroken. There were no prices on either menu and that made Frank more than a little nervous, especially when he saw who was sitting at the table next to them. It was the same two couples who were at the coffee shop where they had lunch that day. During lunch, Frank overheard the guys making a thousand-dollar bet on their golf game. They didn't choke when the bill came, but did have a good laugh over paying seven dollars and fifty cents for a relish tray that consisted of two radishes, two green onions and two carrots.

When they returned from Hawaii, they picked up their new 1980 Firebird they had ordered a few weeks before their trip. It was loaded, including a moon roof. They called it their midlife crisis car. Frank was approaching forty and Marty was right behind him. It was only a year later, when they accepted being middle-aged and bought a new 1981 Lincoln Continental, Mark VI. Frank kept his Firebird, though, for his commute to work.

A few months later, Frank was transferred to work on a job site in Arizona. Their offices were in trailers on the job site in the middle of nowhere. They had port-a-potties and the construction workers threw live rattlesnakes in them when they were not cleaned. Just for fun and to create some excitement, they also threw live Gila Monsters in the beds of the trucks.

Frank flew out every Sunday afternoon to Phoenix, rented a car and drove to Wickenburg. It was a small town where he stayed at a motel near the job site. There were few choices as to where to dine. He flew home every Friday night to the John Wayne Airport in Orange County. Every Sunday when they took Frank to the airport, Buttons chewed Daddy out, talking up a storm, but he would get all excited on Fridays when Mom said, "Let's go pick up Daddy!"

Everything seemed to go wrong when Frank was in Arizona. First Buttons had a heart attack; then his intestines were torn from a tiny chicken bone Marty missed in the chicken she gave him. She had to take Buttons to the vet every day for a pain shot. Marty was a nervous wreck, but he healed very well.

After Frank had been working in Arizona for four and a half months, Marty was trimming plants in the atrium one evening when a jagged leaf caught her left eye, cutting the cornea and damaging the pupil. She thought it was just irritated and would settle down. As the night wore on, the pain and tearing increased until she couldn't see with either eye. She kept thinking, "I can't wake up an eye doctor in the middle of the night; even if I could, I have no way of getting there." She didn't want to disturb her neighbors. So she just spent the night walking the floor, because she couldn't stand the pain when she was sitting or lying down. Early the next morning, she managed to get dressed. It amazed her on how difficult it was when she knew exactly where everything was located. She couldn't see the buttons on the phone, so she dialed "o" to have the operator call the next door neighbor, Russ, for her.

Russ came over immediately and took her to the doctor, guiding her just like a blind person. After examining her eye, Dr. Adrian casually said, "I'm sorry, but I won't know for at least a week if you'll ever see out of this eye again." He put some drops in her eye, applied a patch over it, gave her some pain medication, and said he would need to see her everyday. At least she could see out of the other eye now. After Russ took her home, she called Frank at his office in Arizona. She said, "Don't get excited, but I had an accident with my left eye and I might not see out of it again." Frank said immediately, "I'm coming home; I'll see you tonight and hung up." He told his boss what happened and said, "I'm leaving and I won't be coming back, my wife needs me!" He walked out of the office with his boss yelling, "You can't just leave me like this!" When he got home and told Marty what he did, she was mortified! She thought for sure Bechtel would fire him. Instead, he was assigned to the "United Way Campaign" as a loaned executive until they found a position for him back in the home office.

A few days later, Marty could see, but she had double vision. Dr. Adrian didn't know if the double vision would ever go away, but it did several days later. He told Marty that he was amazed by how fast and how well she had healed. He said, "When you came in that first day, I really didn't think you would ever see out of that eye again, many of my patients don't with that type of injury. You were very fortunate."

After his heart attack, Buttons went down hill fast within a few months and they had to have to put him to sleep. They loved him too much to let him suffer. Frank and Marty clung to each other and sobbed while the vet gave Buttons the shot. Marty didn't know that you could hurt that much inside physically, from emotional pain. They had lost their *child.*

They were not getting another dog, but Marty said to Frank ten days later, "I have to have a baby to love." She found a breeder in the yellow pages and called her the next day. The breeder had a silver gray toy poodle, and it was love at first sight! Toby's personality was totally different than Buttons. Buttons had been their little clown, always pulling something new. But he also had a mind of his own, being stubborn. Toby was all love and eager to please most of the time. When he was a bad boy occasionally, he had a "golly gee whiz" look he gave to Mom that he knew melted her like butter. He got away with murder with that look. Toby and Mom would play for hours with his many toys and Daddy's old socks. He loved playing hide and seek. He would hide and then peek out with a look that said, "Hi Mom, here I am!"

CHAPTER THIRTY-FIVE

Frank's Dad had been dating different ladies for several years and then out of the blue, he called them one night and said, "I'm getting married!" Frank and Marty were thrilled! Dad was like a different person. He was actually happy and enjoyable to be around. Dad and Mary only dated for a few months and got married in Las Vegas. Two days later, they had Thanksgiving dinner with both of their families at Dad's condo. Frank and Marty really hit it off with Mary and her family. They were all great people who were a lot of fun! Mary had two daughters, Eve and Aileen. Eve and her husband Paul had one daughter, Lisa who was divorced with a three year old daughter, Nicky. Mary's other daughter Aileen was married to Don and had no children. Marge was nice and friendly to everyone, but Marty could tell she was putting up a big front. She was jealous and really pissed having to share *her Daddy* with Mary and her family. It was difficult enough for her to just share *her Daddy* with Frank and Marty!

CHAPTER THIRTY-SIX

Marty was having a lot of pain and burning in her feet, so she decided to do something about it. She had both feet operated on, but had no idea what she was getting into. The Podiatrist presented the whole thing to her as if it was no big deal and she bought it. She was using a walker to get around for several months. He put six pins in her feet and eight incisions for bunions, ingrown toe nails, hammer toes and reconstructed her big toes that were twisted. He literally broke the six middle toes and four of them he froze so they could not become hammer toes again. The pins were sticking out of her skin on both ends. It was six months before she could wear regular shoes, after she learned how to walk again by going to therapy every day for weeks. Before the surgery, she told the doctor, "We are taking my Dad on a Caribbean Cruise in seven months for his seventy-fifth Birthday." She then asked, "Should I wait to have this surgery after the cruise?" He said, "No, that's not necessary. You'll be in tip top shape long before that." He lied through his teeth and did not explain all the procedures he was going to do.

Marty had problems on the cruise, and spent a lot of time in their cabin, to rest her feet that were screaming in pain. As it turned out, her feet were just part of the problem on the cruise for dear old Dad. Marty would have never believed it if she hadn't seen it with her own eyes. Her Dad had turned into *a dirty old man*. This solid Christian man from the Bible belt was getting fresh with every single lady he met on the cruise. One lady said to Marty, "You should put a leash on that father of yours!" Marty just replied, "No kidding!" Frank said he wished he had taken the five thousand dollars they spent on the cruise and put it on one roll of the dice on the crap table in Las Vegas. He said it would have been more fun.

They did, however, enjoy the snorkeling on Grand Cayman Island immensely, at two different locations. The water at the first location was fifty feet deep and the instructor asked if there was anyone who didn't know how to swim. Frank told Marty to put up her hand. Marty refused, "If I do, he won't let me off this boat!" Frank grabbed her arm and held it up. The instructor said, "No problem, just come up here for a life jacket." Marty had a ball because with the life jacket, she wasn't afraid and didn't get tired. There were hundreds of beautiful, brilliantly-colored fish. They were so pretty, they almost looked artificial. Frank got confused and swam back to the wrong boat. After he realized it, he had to swim another hundred yards back to their boat and almost didn't make it!

The minute they stopped at the second location, Marty jumped into the water and was off to have more fun. The instructor asked, "Who was that?" Frank said, "My wife." The instructor asked, "The one who doesn't know how to swim?" Frank answered, "Yep! That's her!" He said, "But she didn't give me a chance to tell her that the water is one hundred feet deep now!" He told everyone, "Wave to me if you see a shark. I'll wave back and wish you lots of luck!"

In Jamaica, they took a tour bus to see the beautiful Dunn Falls and had the wildest ride of their lives! The bus driver passed other vehicles on a winding two-way road, laying on horn. They had several very near-misses meeting cars head-on, while rounding curves.

Before and after the cruise, Marty was having severe pains in her chest and the doctor put her in CCU to run tests to find out what was going on with her heart. She was released the day before Thanksgiving. The next day, Frank's dad came up to Marty several times to ask her how she was feeling. She kept telling him, "I'm doing just fine Dad." Every time this happened, Marty caught Marge's look of pure hatred at her because *Marge's Daddy* was showing concern for Marty.

The doctors were unable to find the problem and she had more attacks. She went through six months of Frank calling the paramedics many times. Marty finally got a cardiologist in the ER at the hospital that caught something she told him and decided it was not her heart. They ran every gall bladder test available, but could not even prove she had a gall bladder. The scar Marty had from her stomach surgery was right where the cut would be for gall bladder surgery. They repeatedly asked Marty, "Are you sure they didn't remove your gall bladder in that surgery?" Marty said, "If they did, it was "*oops!*" and didn't tell me." The surgeon who did her stomach surgery had moved out of the state and the hospital where she had the surgery didn't have the records either. Marty said, "I'll sign any damn thing you want that you're not responsible, but please don't make me go through another one of those attacks! You don't know how painful they are, at first you think you are going to die; then you wish you would!" They did the surgery and the doctor said to Marty, "Your gall bladder was packed full of stones, that's why it didn't show up on any of our tests. Many of the stones were large, but some of them were huge! You weren't kidding when you said the pain was unbearable! When you are passing a stone, they go through a very small passage."

Nine days after her gall bladder surgery, Frank and Marty went to Uncle Frank and Aunt Rose's golden wedding anniversary dinner. They were very touched that Marty made such an effort to be there; making a big fuss over the poem she wrote for them in the card and they loved their gift. It was a collectable silver dollar she bought from a coin dealer. It was minted in the year they were married fifty years ago. Marty turned around and again, caught daggers of pure hatred drilling right through her from Marge. Marty thought, "Oh crap, the little darling isn't the center of attention."

CHAPTER THIRTY-SEVEN

Marty became disenchanted with their townhouse. The street behind it had become very busy, and it was difficult for her to sleep with the noise of the traffic. Marty snapped one day and said, "I've had it! We are moving!" She started house hunting in Yorba Linda and found the perfect house in the hills. It had a view of Orange County from Yorba Linda to the ocean. You could see Catalina Island on an occasional clear day; when there wasn't any smog, fog, or haze. Years ago, the Indians called Orange County "Smoky Valley" because of the haze. Marty loved the house and all the open space around it, but the biggest plus was getting away from the traffic noise.

The house wasn't completed yet, but Marty had to drive out to see her house two or three times a week. After a few times, Toby knew where they were going when they got within one mile of the place. He would start chewing Mom out; no barking or whining, but going on and on like he thought he was talking and really telling her what he thought of the place. When that didn't work, and Mom kept going to the stupid place that looked like a barn, Toby marched right into the kitchen and lifted his leg to relieve himself in the middle of the room on the cement slab, looking at Mom right in the eye. The look in his eyes said, "This is what I think of this place, Mom!"

Frank and Marty had signed an agreement with the builder that they would close Escrow upon completion of the house or lose their five thousand dollar deposit, plus lose their option to buy the house. They had the townhouse up for sale, but there were no perspective buyers. The new house was getting close to completion. They did not want to touch their retirement funds to buy the house, so the townhouse had to sell to swing the deal. Frank kept saying to Marty, "I don't think you should be going out to the house so often. It will break your heart if the deal falls through. It's looking more and more unlikely that we will get that house." Marty would reply, "Have faith, Frank! If it is meant to be, it will be! Faith the size of a mustard seed can move mountains!" When the completion of the house was less than thirty days away, Frank said, "Marty, you have to face the facts! Most Escrows are sixty to ninety days and the townhouse has not even sold!" She didn't waver and said, "Frank, have faith!"

The realtors they had signed with to sell the townhouse were not doing a thing. They had not brought anyone by to look at the townhouse and refused to hold an open house, trying to force Marty to lower the price. The realtors felt it was too high, even though real estate had increased a lot and they had made many lavish improvements on the place. Finally Marty told them, "Give me the "Open House" signs and I'll do it myself. Marty got the buyer two weeks before the new house was completed, for more than three times of what they paid for it ten years ago. The buyer put 75 percent cash down and wanted a one week escrow! Frank and Marty took the mortgage personally for the remaining 25 percent. They had their new house in the hills! The real estate company said they never heard of a one week escrow, much less been involved with one. There was no time to mail anything. Marty spent the entire week physically taking all of the papers to different locations for signatures and transfers. The realtors told Marty they were going to give her a very nice gift for finding the buyer. They took eight thousand five hundred and fifty dollars for their commission and Marty received a plant, but she had her new house!

When moving day arrived, Toby had not been out to the new house for a couple of weeks. He walked in and saw the floor with carpet and tile as he saw the movers bringing in "his" furniture. Light bulbs went off in his eyes as it dawned on him, "This is a house and we are going to live here!" He ran around dancing as if to say, "Hey, this is all right!"

Marty set up her subs for bridge and told the girls she would not be at bridge that month because she wouldn't have time with the move and getting settled. One day in the middle of the afternoon, Marty glanced out a window and saw a caravan of cars. All of the girls came by after bridge to surprise Marty and to see her new house. She was a mess and the house was a mess. The girls were in their glory because it always bugged them to no end that Marty's house always looked so perfect!

The landscaping crew put in a large patio, patio cover, fire circle, brick benches, brick planters and brick porches. They also put in retainer walls with wrought iron fences on top. After tilling the soil, they brought in a lot of topsoil, installed the sprinkler system, and landscaped the yards.

In the living room, they extended the river rock on the fireplace up to the cathedral ceiling. The interior was painted in soft green and pale yellow, plus wallpaper was hung throughout the house. She ordered the drapes and everything else to finish decorating. Three months after moving, they hosted the Couples Duplicate Bridge group in their new house. Many more projects came later, but they were basically settled.

After pushing herself before and after the move, Marty got bored after everything was done and signed up with Mary Kay Cosmetics as a consultant. She worked really hard on it, but the profits were not there due to her being too generous with family and friends. A lot of her generosity went to Melody and Terri, Frank's nieces. Occasionally, Marty would have them down before Frank came home from work. They had fun, sitting around the kitchen table with kits, learning new make up techniques. Marty gave them all of their skin care and make up products. After Frank got home, they took the girls out to dinner. Frank would always protest to Marty later, saying they didn't appreciate it, but she would tell him, "Don't spoil my fun; I enjoy giving to the girls!"

The holidays rolled around, and Dad flew out for his annual visit after spending Christmas with Laura and her family in Colorado. He didn't like the fact their property was so open with no privacy. In a fit of temper he said, "Give me a six foot wall so

I can't see out and no one can see in!" Marty took him on a walk around the neighborhood. He asked, "Why didn't you buy one of these big beautiful two-story houses? Doesn't it bother you to be one of the small potatoes of the neighborhood?" Marty replied, "No, it doesn't bother me one bit! In the first place, we couldn't afford one of these big houses. In the second place, why on earth would we want a big two-story house with Frank's leg and my back? Would it kill you, Dad, to show a little pride and happiness for me, just once? Do you realize that you have never said to me once, in my entire life, that you are proud of me?" Dad looked at her in astonishment and said, "What are you talking about? You know I'm proud of you!" Marty answered, "No I don't know that because you have never shown it!" Dad walked into the house in a huff.

CHAPTER THIRTY-EIGHT

Two years later, their whole world turned upside down. Frank was laid off from Bechtel Engineering after fifteen and a half years. The workforce was cut from forty-five hundred people down to eight hundred in Frank's division alone before Frank got the axe. When his boss gave him the news, he said, "I know you won't believe this Frank, but this is more difficult for me than it is for you. You are one of the best and hardest workers we've got! It *kills* me to let you go!"

Frank and Marty saw it coming and saved for it by pulling in their belts drastically. It was devastating for Frank. He didn't just lose a job; he lost his career, his life. Marty joked to other people that it would have been easier for Frank to divorce her than leave Bechtel. California was in a serious recession. Frank got another job right away, but was laid off again, and then he was out of a job for five months.

The holidays came and Melody was getting married on New Year's Eve; Frank and Marty were not invited. Melody came down to see them one evening to explain that since it was her second marriage, she wanted to keep it small and simple. They were hurt and disappointed, but understood.

A couple of weeks later, Frank and Marty had the family down for their traditional Christmas Eve celebration. Marty had beautiful decorations, large Christmas candles glowing, with soft music and a fire in the fireplace. The Christmas tree was an artificial green tree decorated with a lot of care. Marty spent two hours setting the dining room table and a small table in the large entry, covering them with beautiful tablecloths; then setting them with her china and crystal, folding linen napkins in a fancy fashion. Marty served appetizers with drinks when everyone arrived. For dinner she served food that she could fix ahead of time so when everyone arrived, everything was prepared and simmering. When Marge and Dick arrived, the place took on the look of total disaster in five minutes flat! Marge and Dick did not enter a room, they would attack it! Every year Dick would walk in and say, dripping in sarcasm, "You call that a Christmas tree?"

On this Christmas Eve, Marge spent the entire evening rubbing Marty's nose in it about the wedding and the fact they were not invited. When everyone opened Christmas gifts in Frank's family, they took turns opening one gift at a time and repeatedly went around the room until everyone had opened every gift. This way, the gift opening wasn't over in twenty minutes. Dad took Marge shopping every year before Christmas to buy her gifts. Every gift Marge opened from Dad; she turned to Marty and said with a childish grin on her face and announced in her snotty way, "This is for the wedding!" Dick started throwing balls of wrapping paper across the living room, just barely missing Marty's expensive liqueur set on the coffee table.

Frank and Marty blew up at Marge and Dick after the holidays and didn't see them for six months. Then Marge called and asked if they could meet at a restaurant to talk things out. They got into it all over again in the restaurant. Marty felt the only reason they were not thrown out of the restaurant is because they were amusing all the other customers too much. Frank and Marty finally agreed to forget the whole thing like they did many times in the past, but they did not have Christmas Eve again. They told the family, we will be with you on Christmas day but not Christmas Eve and we will not exchange gifts in the future. (Marty never understood why they all had to be together for both Christmas Eve and Christmas Day anyway.) Frank and Marty had Easter, Father's Day, and Dad's Birthday. Marge had Thanksgiving and Christmas Day. Sometimes one of Mary's daughters had Thanksgiving for everyone on both sides, but usually the two sides had their holiday dinners separately. Frank and Marty had both sides a couple of times on Easter. She also included Uncle Frank and Aunt Rose for Dad's Birthday parties plus a few times on Easter when they didn't have other plans.

Aunt Rose would say something once in a while from way out in left field. Sometimes you wondered if she had a few short circuits. One Easter Aunt Rose started telling everyone at the dinner table, "Frank is a wonderful lover! He is so thoughtful! He is such a wonderful lover!" Uncle Frank was ninety years old at the time and Aunt Rose was eighty-two. Uncle Frank turned red in the face and looked like he wanted to crawl under the table! Finally, he said to her, "That's enough Rose!" She continued, "But it's true! It's true! He is a won-der-ful lover!"

Several months later when they were celebrating Dad's birthday, Marty was sitting on the sofa with Aunt Rose and asked her how Uncle Frank was doing with his heart. (He had been having problems.) She said, "Oh, he's just fine, honey, he's just fine. We have a very active sex life you know!" Marty said, "Excuse me?" Aunt Rose answered, "Oh yes, that's very important for good health!"

Later on in the fall, Lisa got married again. Lisa's grandmother, Mary, was also Frank's stepmother. Lisa was a drop dead gorgeous girl! She had looks, brains, personality and a perfect little petite body too! At twenty-seven years old, she married a sixty-eight year old man who was very wealthy. He had a big beautiful house in Arcadia at the foot of the mountains. Lisa spent money like crazy on the house, her clothes and jewelry. Her dressing room looked like a small dress shop, with hats on a rack, drawers and drawers of clothes, and dozens of beautiful gowns and dresses. Victor, her husband, had a workout room with a tanning bed put in for her. He didn't want her to go to the gym or tanning salon like a commoner. Lisa was a very hard worker and spent a lot of her time doing charity work.

One year after Lisa and Victor were married, they invited everyone on both sides of the family for Thanksgiving. By then she had completely redecorated the entire house. It was a show place! Lisa was truly a gourmet cook and had a beautiful kitchen fit for a professional chef. After dinner, in the course of conversation, Lisa's husband mentioned his mafia buddies. He saw Marty's eyebrows shoot up and he just looked at her with a smile and winked. Frank and Marty talked about it on the way home. Is he or isn't he? He certainly looked mafia.

Right out of the blue one day, Aunt Rose said to Mary, "Your granddaughter is a whore! She is an expensive call girl with a marriage license!" Mary never went to Aunt Rose's house again. Dad had to go see his brother alone every week.

CHAPTER THIRTY-NINE

Frank went through three years of working a few months here and a few months there, with months in between with no income except the small unemployment checks. Finally, he landed a job with Parsons, another big construction firm like Bechtel. He was working long hours in a trailer on the job site, plus commuting over three hours every day, but he was doing well. The title of his new position was, "Principal Project Control Engineer."

One evening while he was sitting in his recliner watching TV, he grabbed his chest. Marty caught it and asked, "What's the matter?" He said, "It's nothing." Marty then said, "Don't give me that, you are having chest pains. When did this start?" Frank replied, "A few days ago." Marty ran to the phone. Frank yelled at her, "Don't make that call! I'm not going to the hospital! It has stopped now and I am fine!" She didn't want to upset him, so she came back to the living room and said, "I'll not make that call on one condition. Tomorrow morning, you are not going to work. You are going in to see my doctor." Frank agreed.

Marty called her doctor the next morning and he said, "Bring him in immediately." Frank didn't even have a doctor at the time. He never went unless he had a problem. He didn't want Marty to take him, so he went alone. Marty was afraid of pushing; he might not go at all then. She waited anxiously until he came home, but deep down she really didn't expect it to be anything serious. Other than his bad leg, Frank was healthy as a horse. He never had anything except an occasional cold. She was the one who seemed to always have a problem.

When Frank came home, he looked at her like someone had just punched him in the gut. He said, "The doctor suspects that I have heart disease! I have to go to the hospital for tests!" Marty was dumbfounded; you could have pushed her over with a feather. She walked over to give him a hug and stood there holding him, saying, "We've been through a lot, Babe, and we'll get through this one too. Remember what we have said many times over the years, "We can get through anything as long as we have each other and God guiding our way."

Frank was admitted in Brea Community Hospital for tests, and then they sent him to St. Jude's Hospital in Fullerton. He had an angiogram and then underwent an angioplasty the same day on two arteries to his heart. One had a greater than 90 percent obstruction and the other one had a 70 percent obstruction. Dr. Marsh, the cardiologist, explained to Marty that Frank was very fortunate to have had the warning signs of pain, many people don't; they have a heart attack and are gone.

Marty called Marge from the hospital after the angiogram to let her know they were performing the angioplasty that afternoon. Marge, Dick and Dad came down to sit with Marty during the surgery. Mary didn't come because she wasn't feeling well. When they were rolling Frank away for surgery, Dad walked over to Marty and put his arm around her to give her moral support. Marge immediately came over to squeeze in to be next to *her Daddy*. While they were waiting, Marty asked Dad if he wanted to go outside for a smoke—he hated hospitals and had ants in his pants. He jumped up at the suggestion and was out of there! While Marty had her cigarette and Dad had his pipe, she could see Marge through the glass doors out of the corner of her eye. Marty was getting daggers of pure hatred, because she had *Marge's Daddy* all to herself.

Dr. Marsh came into the waiting room and Marty walked over to him to get his report with everyone else behind her. The surgeon told them everything went very well, but the next forty-eight hours were critical because so many things could go wrong during that period of time. In two days, if everything went well, they would put Frank in a regular room. Then they would send him home the following day. In four days, he would be back to work. Marge walked up to Dr. Marsh, getting right into his face, and asked in her loud irritating voice as if he was hard of hearing, "Did he have a heart attack?" The surgeon immediately stepped back, giving Marge a look that asked, "Who in the hell are you?" He then answered slowly, "No, he didn't." Marge turned around to Marty and said, "See! That's why Frank gets to go back to work so soon! He didn't even have a heart attack! Dick had a heart attack and couldn't go back to work for six weeks! Dick had muscle damage!" Dick gave Marge a dirty look and said to Marty, "I had a mild heart attack and very little muscle damage that healed with no problem." The poor surgeon took off and Marty didn't say a word. She stood there praying, "Please, dear Lord, give me strength! Why does she have to make a contest out of everything, even this?"

Frank came through the whole thing like a champ! He was back to work that Friday. His diet and habits had to change, plus he was on several medications, but he was doing great!

CHAPTER FORTY

One year after Frank had a close call with his heart, they celebrated their Silver Wedding Anniversary. They had talked about going to Hawaii to celebrate, but Marty thought it would be more fun to go to Las Vegas where they went on their honeymoon. It was the first time in fifteen years since they had been to Las Vegas. It was in 1977 when they were there and saw the shooting at the Aladdin Casino; Marty swore she never wanted to go again.

Marty booked a room at the Mirage. She told them they were arriving on their twenty-fifth wedding anniversary. When they checked in, the Mirage had upgraded their room to an upper deluxe with a beautiful view of the strip and volcano. There was a big basket of fruit, nuts, and goodies in the room to welcome them. Later that evening, they had their anniversary dinner at Kokomos, a beautiful restaurant in the middle of the rain forest. The décor made them feel like they were in Hawaii. The service was outstanding as they were pampered with pinacoladas, fantastic food and sinful deserts. The filets were so good and tender, each bite melted in their mouths. While they were dining, Frank realized he didn't have the room key and was afraid he had left it in the door when they left the room. Frank told the waiter, and they posted a security guard outside their room while they dined. A few minutes later, Frank found the key in his shirt pocket and they removed the security guard. Kokomos had a professional photographer who took their picture. It was great to have the picture in memory of their big celebration even though Frank looked a little pie-eyed.

After the wonderful dinner, Frank and Marty gambled for a couple of hours before retiring for the night. When they entered their room, there was a nice bottle of champagne, chilling in a sterling silver bucket with champagne glasses. The bed was turned down with an orchid on Marty's pillow and chocolates on both of their pillows.

The view was breathtaking from their room! They could see the beautiful lights of the strip and the dramatic eruption of the volcano. Neither one of them felt any pain at that point, so they saved the champagne to take home with them.

Everything was absolutely perfect! They fell in love with the Mirage, and from that day forward, the Mirage was their place!

CHAPTER FORTY-ONE

One morning, just seconds before Frank's alarm went off at 4:30 a.m., the bed started doing its own rumba. They were having another earthquake. Toby snuggled up to Mom for protection. It seemed to last for a long time, not like most of the tremors they had that were over in a few seconds. Marty knew that usually meant somewhere there was a lot of damage. The second it was over, she jumped out of bed and ran to the living room to turn on the TV to find out the central location of the quake. The TV didn't have any picture or sound, just static. The crystal chandelier that hung over the dining room table was swinging back and forth several feet. Marty made a quick visual check around the house. Many things were out of place but everything seemed to be okay. She went outside to check the gas meter and she could smell a small gas leak.

After calling the gas company, she ran back to the bedroom. Frank was standing calmly in front of his sink in the master dressing room, shaving. In front of him was a large mirror over the vanity and behind him was the glass enclosing the shower.

After a bad earthquake, there are always many aftershocks that can be even worse than the quake itself. They always warn people on the news to stay away from glass that can shatter after an earthquake.

Marty asked him, "What do you think you are doing?" Frank answered, "What's it look like I'm doing? I'm getting ready to go to work." Marty said, "Frank, what is the matter with you? We just had a bad earthquake and I can't even get a picture or sound on the TV! If the TV stations are down, then that means the L.A. area got it really bad! You don't even know if your family's okay! Your office is in that area! You're not going to work!" Frank answered nonchalantly, "Oh Marty, the world doesn't stop going around just because we have an earthquake." She said, "It's still pitch black out there! You could drive over a power line that is down or drive off an overpass that has collapsed because you wouldn't be able to see the problem ahead of you!" He said, "I'm going to work!" Marty then said, "If you insist on going, you are not leaving here until daybreak so you can see any problems ahead of you, and you are going to call me the minute you get there!" He agreed reluctantly.

Marty finally got TV reception and the center of the quake was in Northridge, near the city of L.A., and was indeed a bad one! When Frank called her from work, he said he couldn't believe the damage he saw and his office was a mess. One overpass collapsed and a policeman died driving off of it in the dark. One of the guys Frank worked with lived in Northridge. Their house was demolished and they lost everything! However, the important thing was everyone in their family was okay.

The gas company came and fixed the gas leak on the meter, plus checked for leaks under ground and around the whole neighborhood. Frank's family had minor damage on their homes and no one was hurt. His family lived about twenty miles east of L.A. The TV on top of the high chest in Marge and Dick's bedroom moved and almost fell off when they had a big aftershock. Marge had just walked by the TV two minutes before. After she told the story a few times, the TV *did* fall off the chest, *right on her back!* Her husband Dick called her on it and said, "It did not!" Her answer was, "Well, it could have!" This was so typical of Marge, making up stories to get sympathy from everyone.

They announced on the news, "In the next forty-eight hours, there is a fifty-fifty chance of aftershocks stronger than the earthquake itself, which would cause more catastrophic damage." Frank and Marty had tickets for the "Phantom of the Opera" at the Music Center in L.A. the next day. They decided to go in spite of the situation. Marty became more and more uptight as they got closer to L.A. Frank reached over and touched her arm to tell her to relax and said, "My God, your arm is stiff as a board!" They arrived at the Music Center and parked inside their garage. Marty looked up and saw nothing but tons and tons of concrete that could collapse on them.

Their seats in the balcony were steep to give everyone a good view of the stage. Marty held on tightly to the arms of her chair. Frank kept telling her, "Relax! Nothing is going to happen!" The music was beautiful and the costumes were gorgeous!

Afterwards, it took thirty minutes to get out of the building with everyone leaving at once. As they were waiting for traffic to move out of the garage; Marty said to Frank, "Look at all that concrete. If we have a strong aftershock and this place comes down, don't let me live and be trapped in it for hours or days. Frank kept telling her, "Just relax, nothing is going to happen!" After they got on the freeway and were well on their way home, Frank said, "Okay, I can come clean with you now. I was so terrified that something was going to happen, I couldn't even enjoy that beautiful music!"

CHAPTER FORTY-TWO

Terri, Frank's niece, called to tell them her big news! Rick and Terri were expecting a baby and getting married. They had been living together for some time. When everyone came to Frank and Marty's for Easter a week later, Marty decided this was the time to break out the champagne they brought home from their silver wedding anniversary celebration in Las Vegas. After everyone arrived and Marty was serving the hors d'oeuvres, Frank popped the cork, poured everyone a glass and made a toast to the happy couple and the little one on the way!

Rick and Terri had a lovely garden wedding in Marge and Dick's back yard. Frank and Marty gave them a very nice check in a beautiful card knowing they needed money more than anything else. A couple of weeks before Thanksgiving, they had a beautiful baby boy. Marge called Marty to tell her as soon as they got home from the hospital. Marty told her they would come up to the hospital that night when Frank got home from work. Marge said, "Don't go up to Terri's room until we get there! Wait for us down in the lobby!" Then she said it six more times, "Don't go up to Terri's room until we get there! Wait for us down in the lobby!" Frank and Marty arrived at the hospital and waited for forty-five minutes before Marge and Dick arrived. Frank was upset that Marty had promised her they would not go up without them. He had been up since 4:30 a.m. and had spent three and a half hours on the road going to and from work before driving one hour to the hospital. He had nothing to eat all day but cookies and an apple with a ton of coffee. They still had to go out to eat and drive another hour back home.

Marge and Dick finally arrived and they all went up to Terri's room. She had the baby in the room with her. Marty started to walk into the room, but Dick's arm shot out and he literally shoved Marty out of the way, saying, "Grandma's first!" Frank and Marty waited in the hall for another twenty minutes while Marge went in and Dick did his thing with the video camera. Finally, they were allowed to go in to see Terri and little Michael.

Terri was a picture of contentment! Seeing Michael in his mother's arms moved Marty so much spiritually, she wrote a poem about it later that night when she got home.

Marty came out of the room and said to everyone, "He is beautiful! We have to go eat dinner now. We will see you all on Thanksgiving." Marge told them, "Go downstairs, but don't leave until we come down." Frank and Marty waited another twenty minutes, then said to each other, "The hell with this—let's go!"

Marge told Marty on the phone a few days later that Rick, Terri, and Michael would not be there on Thanksgiving because they were having Rick's family over for dinner that evening. Marty called Terri and asked if they could stop by to bring Michael's gifts after leaving Marge and Dick's. Terri said, "We would love it Aunt Marty!"

When everyone was leaving Marge and Dick's, Marty mentioned they were stopping at Terri's on the way home. Dick had a fit! He asked Marge in Marty's presence over and over, "Why are they going over there Marge? Marge, why are they going over there?" Finally Marge said, "Its okay. They called Terri and asked if it was okay." Marty wanted to scream! Did they need Marge and Dick's permission to go see the kids?"

Rick and Terri were thrilled they came and loved the gifts. They bought Michael a solid 14 karat gold rope chain and gold cross to wear after he was grown because the size of the chain and cross was for a man. Marty also had the spiritual poem she composed on Michael's birth hand written professionally and presented it in a beautiful frame. She bought a little romper outfit too. Terri thought the poem was the most beautiful and touching thing she had ever read. Frank and Marty got to hold their beautiful baby boy!

A couple of weeks later, one of Marge's friends had a "grandma shower" for her. Marty never heard of such a thing and didn't go. By now, Marty was fed up with their parade of becoming grandparents. She felt Marge and Dick were acting like Michael's birth was their show and were stealing Rick and Terri's thunder. They had Michael's picture on throw pillows, hats, T-shirts, coffee mugs, key rings, and large metal buttons to wear on their clothing. It was unbelievable!

Frank and Marty stopped in to see Dad and Mary one day and saw their neighbors who were also in Marge and Dick's camping group. Marty cracked up when the neighbor made the comment, "Marge and Dick think they are the first couple to become grandparents since Adam and Eve!"

One evening, Marge and Dick came down to go out to dinner. They were all sitting on the patio having drinks when Dick started in, "You have no idea what you are missing not having grandkids! You have no idea! It is the most wonderful thing in the world! I wouldn't have missed it for anything! You have no idea what you are missing! It is so great! He went on and on! Marty just sat there biting her lip, trying to keep it shut. She wanted so badly to ask, "Do you enjoy being cruel or are you so damn dumb that you don't realize how rude and cruel you are to us?"

Occasionally, when Marty did speak up, Marge and Dick would either deny what they had said or say they were just kidding. Then they would accuse Marty of trying to create problems out of nothing and being a trouble maker. She was always in the wrong.

After nearly twenty years, Marty resigned as Bridge Chairman and quit playing entirely because she came home after bridge with splitting headaches. She thought she would miss it, but didn't feel a thing but relief. The phone wasn't ringing with someone saying, "I can't make it to bridge and I can't find a sub; will you do it for me?" This happened all the time. When someone couldn't hostess when they were scheduled to, Marty stepped in and had bridge at her house, in addition to having her own turn as hostess. The girls were not calling anymore with their petty complaints about each other or the subs.

Marty was busy with projects on the house. Frank was still working very long hours, on top of his long commute every day. Toby was her little buddy and they had a lot of time together. Frank bought Marty a computer with a printer and he taught her how to operate it. She made up her own format for their retirement charts which covered the next twenty-five years. The charts had all of their accounts, with average percentages of interest every year for growth; their income, less expenses, with cost of living increases each year on the expenses allowing for inflation; plus making entries for taxes after she worked out what the federal and state taxes would be for each year. She put in extra expenses for the years they planned to buy a car, also for upkeep and decorating the house. She updated her budget every month and the charts at least once a year.

Melody and Bob bought a big beautiful house in Diamond Bar, a lovely area in the hills. Marty wanted to do something very special for their housewarming gift since she had done so much for Terri when she had her baby. Marty tried to keep things even in giving to Frank's nieces. She asked Melody for ideas and she wanted silk trees and plants for the large shelf by their staircase landing. Melody and Bob went shopping with her and they had a ball going to several places to find top quality silks. After they bought the silks and got them home, Marty spent the rest of the day arranging and fine tuning them. After two Saturdays of shopping and arranging, they were complete. One Saturday, Frank helped paint their master bathroom and walk-in closet. Frank also brought them several flats of baby tears from their own yard and helped Bob plant them.

Since Marty wasn't in bridge anymore and not having Christmas Eve, she didn't need her good china. When they entertained friends or had family dinners now, they had a simple BBQ with steaks. Marty used her stoneware for that and not her good china. When she was working on the silk plants at Melody's, she observed that her china would be perfect with

Melody's décor. The floor was silver gray marble in their large entry and dining room, and the carpet was light silver blue in the living room. Bob and Melody bought a beautiful dining room table and hutch with ten chairs in cherry wood. Marty's china was white with a silver gray pattern and a tiny bit of red. Marty asked Melody if she would like to have her china and Melody was thrilled! The china was made in Western Germany and in perfect condition—not a scratch, no chips or fading. It had cost thirty-two dollars per place setting in 1964. Marty had twelve place settings, plus the meat platter, gravy bowl, vegetable bowl, sugar and creamer. She had invested six hundred dollars in buying everything over several years, and it was worth much more than that now. Marty gave Melody all the certificates for the china, which guaranteed that replacements would always be available.

She also gave Melody and Terri many lovely pieces of her 14 karat gold jewelry. A lot of gold jewelry and expensive clothes were not important to Marty now since their lifestyle had changed drastically. No more bridge and they didn't have all the formal occasions they had with BEC when Frank worked for Bechtel Engineering. There were many other lovely items she gave to the girls. Since Melody was getting Marty's china, Marge gave Mom's china to Terri she had been saving for the girls since Mom died.

After Frank and Marty went to Las Vegas to celebrate their silver wedding anniversary, they started going three to four times a year, and always stayed at the Mirage. Bob and Melody said they would like to go with them on their next trip. Marty and Melody set up the dates and they stayed at the Mirage in upper deluxe rooms. One night, they had dinner at Kokomos by the rain forest in the Mirage. (The OJ Simpson murder trial was in session at the time in Los Angeles.) When they commented on the size of their steak knives, the waiter said they were OJ knives. Everyone laughed and after the waiter walked away, Marty said to Bob, "I wonder what his reaction would have been if I told him that LAPD was sitting here at our table." Bob replied, "Don't you dare!" Bob was very low keyed about being on the L.A. police force. Melody was a school teacher for high school mathematics. During the summer, she taught teachers how to teach. Bob and Melody did very well. Their Uncle Frank and Aunt Marty were very proud of them. They all had a fabulous time!

Melody loved the silks that Marty had arranged so much that she asked Marty to make an arrangement to cover the top of her hutch. Marty told her, "I would love to, just give me a date." When Marty arrived at their house, Melody proudly showed her the china in her hutch on display. The china was perfect with Melody's décor. Their house was shaping up just beautifully. They had asked Frank and Marty for ideas on what to do with the landscaping and that was looking gorgeous too. Bob was a very hard worker and had good taste for the finer things in life. Melody told Marty, "I have to tell you what Bob said to me, 'I want you to let Aunt Marty do whatever she wants, she knows what she is doing.' Aunt Marty, Bob wouldn't say that about another person in the entire world!" Marty spent the afternoon going up and down the eight foot ladder and the staircase a hundred times to get the plants perfect from every angle. You could see the top of the hutch coming down the stairs. They loved it! Melody was concerned about how sore Marty would be the next day. Marty didn't tell her it would be more like a week. She asked Marty if she would make arrangements for other places in the house. Marty told her, "I would love it! Just let me know when you have time to go shopping." Melody had them stay for dinner and they had a lovely evening together.

Terri and her little family came down occasionally and they took them out to dinner. Marty always told them, "Order anything you want; it's our treat." Terri had another beautiful baby boy, Matthew. Aunt Marty composed another spiritual poem and had it professionally written and framed beautifully. She did everything the same as she did for Michael, except this time Frank and Marty waited a couple of weeks to go up to see them. Frank said he wasn't going to the hospital to see Dick and Marge's production number on becoming grandparents again.

Marty should have seen it coming, but she didn't have a clue! Marge called Marty and announced that she was no longer having Thanksgiving dinners. They were starting a new family tradition. Terri and Rick were having it every year for the immediate family only. Frank and Marty were on their own, this Thanksgiving and all future Thanksgivings!

Two weeks after Thanksgiving, Bob and Melody had a family "Christmas Brunch" on Marty's china, surrounded by the silk trees and plants Marty had worked on for three days, not counting the days she spent planning it all out in her mind and drawing it out on paper to scale. Frank and Marty were not invited. They were not supposed to know about the brunch, but Mary spilled the beans. Dad jumped all over Mary for opening her mouth. Mary said, "I'm sorry, but I think they have a right to know!"

There was smell of a dead rat in the air, named Marge! Marty was beginning to see a pattern. Every time she got close to the girls over the years, Marge always managed to have something happen to cause a riff between them. Marge was an expert liar and manipulator to have her own way. She could not handle Marty having a close relationship with the girls. In a very sick way, Dick and Marge considered their daughters and grandsons as their own private property. Their jealousy toward Frank and Marty went far deeper than they ever dreamed. The one thing that Marge and Dick had over Frank and Marty was having kids and grandkids, and they took sheer delight in rubbing their noses in it. They did not want Frank and Marty to be part of the family. They just wanted them to be spectators for their shows.

Marty called Marge and asked her about the brunch. Marge said, "You were not invited because Melody can only seat ten people around her dining room table." Marty told her, "Oh and God forbid if she set up a card table covered with a small table cloth in her entry like I've done for years to make room for your family!"

Frank and Marty were certain that the new Thanksgiving tradition idea did not come from Terri. It had the smell of Marge and Dick all over it! They also knew that Melody probably made the comment to her mom about the problem with the seating arrangement for her Christmas Brunch and Marge undoubtedly said, "Don't invite Frank and Marty. They'll never know."

CHAPTER FORTY-THREE

Marty called her Dad to chat and could tell his breathing was labored. He had a bad fall on a job and fractured a couple of ribs. He put on his back brace and was taking it easy. Marty told him, "Dad, you really need to see your doctor so he can take x-rays." He finally went and they gave him a shot for the pain right in his rib cage. Marty talked to him that night and he was feeling much better, but he went downhill very rapidly the next five days. The last two days, Byron went over after work and stayed with Dad all night. He tried to get Dad to go to the hospital, but he would not budge. Saturday morning Dad told Byron, "Okay, it's time for me to go to the hospital, but no damn ambulance." He didn't want people to see the inside of his house. Lucky for Byron, Aunt Lula and Uncle Guy arrived a few minutes later. Aunt Lula helped Byron get him to the car. Uncle Guy used a walker to get around and wasn't able to help.

Byron called when Marty was on her way out the door for her regular hair appointment. He told her, "Dad is on his deathbed, I don't think he will last long." Marty said immediately, "I'm coming home. I'll call you later, after I schedule my flight." She found Frank in the back yard weeding, and told him, "Dad is on his death bed. I have to fly back to Kansas. I'm leaving now for my hair appointment." She took off, leaving Frank standing there with a shocked look on his face. The minute she got home, she called the hospital, even though Byron told her that Dad couldn't talk. They rang Dad's room and the nurse answered the phone. Marty told the nurse who she was and ask her to hold the phone to her dad's ear. She said, "Daddy, I love you and I'm coming home. I'll see you tomorrow." Dad tried to remove the oxygen mask to talk to her but she couldn't understand him. The nurse took the phone and told her, "He's trying to tell you that he loves you too."

Marty asked Frank if he would go with her, but he said it couldn't have happened at a worse time for him at the office. He had a lot of "irons in the fire" for the entire week and a meeting with the Assistant Mayor of Los Angeles. The city of Los Angeles was their client of the project.

When Marty called the airlines, she explained the situation and asked for the first flight out to Kansas City. The best connection she could get was leaving LAX at six-thirty the next morning with a lay over in Houston. She called Byron at work and his boss, Barbara, answered the phone. She said he had left the office for a family emergency. Marty told Barbara who she was and asked, "Dad's gone, isn't he?" Barbara hesitated, and then said softly, "Yes, he is." Marty called the hospital and asked for Dad's room. Laura had arrived from Colorado twenty minutes before Dad died. Byron and Laura were still in the room with him. Marty talked to both of them briefly, then told Byron, "I'll call you later at home."

There was one more phone call that Marty had to make before she could start packing for her trip. Dad and Mildred's relationship had changed, but they were very close for twenty years. Mildred's health had deteriorated badly and she was moved to a convalescent hospital in Missouri to be near her son and his family.

When Marty made the call to Mildred and told her Dad was gone, her immediate reaction was relief. Mildred said, "I worried so much about his welfare." Marty knew exactly what Mildred was trying to say because she felt the same way. Dad was eighty-six years old and had no savings or social security; nothing but two dilapidated old houses full of crap and fifteen junky old cars that Dad called his *cream puffs*. The only things he had of any value were his antique furniture, guns and clocks. Marty sent him money many times over the years, but it would have been very difficult to pay three thousand dollars a month for his care in a convalescent home for any length of time. Dad had a deep hatred for convalescent homes anyway. He was also dead set against living with any one of his kids—not that Marty could have handled having him living with her and Frank. After having him there for two weeks on his annual visits, she was a basket case. It would have been a hopeless situation. Marty knew she worried about him, but didn't realize how much until it dawned on her that she didn't have to worry about him anymore and felt like the whole world had been lifted off her shoulders. He was in heaven now with Mama.

Byron's son, Brent, was living in Kansas City at the time. He picked Marty up at the airport and took her to Larned with him and his fiancée, Faith. On the way to Larned, Brent said he didn't want to stay at his dad's. He asked Marty how much it would cost for them to stay at the motel where she had reservations. She told them they were welcome to share her motel room with her, and they were happy to accept the offer. Marty had asked Byron to make reservations for her at the Best Western Motel when she called him with her flight information. She wasn't about to stay in Dad's crappy house stuffed full of all his *treasures* and Byron's guest room in his mobile home was a storage room.

They arrived in Larned at 1:00 a.m. and called Byron as soon as they checked into their motel room. He wanted them to let him know when they arrived regardless of how late it was. Byron came over to their motel room and they talked until 5:00 a.m. While they were chatting, Marty looked out the window. She said, "Hey guys, there's a hearse parked out there right in front of our room! Dad came over to check up on us!" They all laughed and said, "Yeah, right!" Marty explained to Faith, "When we were growing up, Dad never hired a sitter, but we never knew when he would show up and catch us off guard."

Brent and Faith seemed to be a perfectly matched pair. Marty was thrilled to see how Faith had brought Brent out of his shell that he had been in since his mother and little sister were killed in the car accident when Brent was seven years old. It was great to see Brent so happy.

It was 10:00 a.m. before they got up that morning. After they got ready, they went over to pick up Byron. When they walked into his front door, he was on the phone with Laura and he was so upset that he was red in the face. They were arguing about the pallbearers. Marty told him loud enough so Laura could hear her, "Byron, hang up! I'm here now and you're not taking that crap!" Byron turned to Marty and said, "She just hung up on me!" Marty said, "Okay guys, this is the plan. When we go over to Dad's house, if Laura starts getting on our case; we are going to just turn around and walk out of there!"

They left to go eat breakfast at the Harvest Inn and had just sat down, when Aunt Lula and Uncle Guy walked in looking for them. They chatted a bit; then Uncle Guy and Aunt Lula left to go home. A few minutes later Diana, Laura's daughter, walked in alone. After they all had their hugs and greetings she said, "Mom wants to know when you guys are coming over to Grandpa's house. Everyone else is there." Marty answered her, "Tell your mom we'll be over when we get around to it." Diana replied, "Mom didn't mean to fly off the handle, she is so tired." Marty told her, "Diana, that's just the way your mom is and she will never change. All of us are tired. Byron didn't see a bed for three days until five o'clock this morning. I didn't see a bed Saturday night and we just got to bed at five o'clock this morning too. We are just now having breakfast; then we are going over to the mortuary to see Dad." Diana asked, "Can I go with you to the mortuary?" Marty told her, "Of course!"

When they walked out of the Harvest Inn, Diana put her arm around Marty and asked if she would ride to the mortuary with her. Marty told the others, "We'll meet you there." Diana and Kevin had been married for seventeen years and had two great kids. They started out so young with nothing and worked very hard over the years. Marty was so proud of them. It had been nineteen years since Marty had been to Colorado, but Diana, Kevin, and the kids came to California several times on vacation.

Marty walked into the mortuary and was shocked when she saw her Dad. He was eighty-six years old, but he always looked young for his age because he was so active. Up until his bad fall a few weeks ago, Dad was still working and bowling every week in a league. Dad was very thin now and looked so frail. She asked Byron about it and he told her Dad had lost all the weight just since his fall. The tears started rolling down her face. She couldn't believe he was gone.

After leaving the mortuary, they went over to Dad's house to face the music. Marty had no idea what kind of reception she would get from her sister, Laura. They had not had much of a relationship or even seen each other for nineteen years. When they walked into the house, everyone was happy to see her! Diana offered to take Marty's mink jacket right away. Marty looked around at all the crap and thought to herself, "Take it where?" Not wanting to appear like the snob Laura always said she was, Marty just said, "No thank you, I'll keep it on. I've been cold ever since I got here."

The wallpaper on the wall was pealing and hanging down. Part of the ceiling was hanging down too. Laura had cleared out all the junk in the living room and cleaned it so people coming in would have a place to sit, but the rest of the place was so full of crap, there were just paths to walk through the house.

Laura came up to Marty and gave her a big hug. She said, "It's so great to see you." Marty turned around from greeting everyone else and Delorse, her oldest sister who lived in San Antonio was standing there with a big smile waiting to give her a hug too. She was so sweet, but always so wrapped up in her church, even above caring for her children or doing her housework when they were growing up. Years ago, Marty tried telling her that God didn't put those kids in her care to neglect them by putting her church activities first, but no light bulbs went off. Delorse and Earl bought a farm and rented out their house in town before their divorce twenty-five years ago. In the divorce settlement, Earl received full custody of the children and she got the house in town. The mortgage on her house was almost paid in full. She turned right around and gave the house to her church. Dad, who was furious with Earl at the time of the divorce said, "She thinks she just bought herself a first class ticket to Heaven. Boy, is she in for a surprise, because that is one place you can't buy your way into!"

Delorse's daughter, Pam, was there with her husband and six year old daughter. Pam's husband was a deep-sea skin diver who made underwater repairs on offshore oil wells in Louisiana.

Vernon, Delorse's oldest son who also lived in San Antonio, could not come because he was in charge of taking care of his three small children while his wife was in Florida for her own grandfather's funeral. Vernon worked for the Federal Government and was doing very well in his career. After returning from Vietnam, he worked full time while going to night school. He not only graduated from college, but continued until he got his Masters.

Tom, Delorse's second son, did not come because no one notified him. He was a mess beyond belief! He was the one who slept with his brother's first wife when his brother was in Vietnam. Later, Tom joined the marines and was stationed at Camp Pendleton in Southern California. Marty tried to put him on the right path in life during the time he lived in California, but he was a hopeless case. He went AWOL twice and got his girl, Cookie, pregnant who was scum. When he went on leave, he took Cookie to Colorado and tried to dump her on his Aunt Laura's door step. Aunt Laura told him, "You're not leaving her here. You got her pregnant, she's your problem!"

He took Cookie to Kansas and left her at his mom's house, and went out to see his old girlfriend from his high school days, Mona. She still lived with her parents on their farm. Cookie suspected that he went to see Mona, the girl he had told her about months ago. She talked Delorse into taking her there by saying, "If you don't, I'll walk out there." She couldn't let Cookie walk several miles in the heat, being eight months pregnant.

It didn't occur to Delorse that Cookie wouldn't even know how to get there. She was never the sharpest knife in the drawer.

Tom and Mona were all wrapped up in each other on a blanket, in the front yard when Delorse and Cookie drove up in the car. Cookie, big as a house from being pregnant, grabbed an empty pop bottle on the floor of Delorse's car, jumped out of the car and started hitting Tom with the bottle. She screamed at him, "You stupid son of a bitch! How could you do this do me? I'm carrying your fucking baby!" Mona's parents heard all the yelling and came running out of the house. They yelled at Tom, "You get off of our property and never come back! Don't you ever step foot on our property again!"

But Tom did go back, the next day, and he not only talked his way back into the good graces of Mona's parents, but he married Mona four days later—with their blessings! Tom was a good looking guy and could charm his way out of anything. In fact, he bragged about that fact once to Marty. Her reply was, "And you think that's something to be proud of?" He put Cookie on a plane back to California—she was on her own with a baby on the way. Tom and Mona were married for nearly twenty years and had three kids. They beat up on each other and had a very stormy marriage. Then Tom left Mona and moved in with three strippers he met at a strip club. Over the years, he ripped off several people in the family; some for hundreds of dollars and others for thousands.

A man who looked like a *Hells Angel* walked into Dad's house. Marty asked Diana, "Who is that guy who just walked in the door?" Diana said, "That's my brother Roy." Marty thought, "No way!" She then asked Diana, "Who is the gal with Roy?" Diana made a face and said, "Tanya!" Marty replied, "Tanya! What is she doing here?" Diana answered, "That's what you and everyone else would like to know!" As it turned out, Tanya drove her husband Roy there because he lost his driver's license after being picked up on a DUI three times! They had their son Matthew with them. He was her son anyway; everyone else had their doubts whether he belonged to Roy. Marty thought they were divorced, but they were just separated when Roy moved back home. Tanya was living with another guy and they both lost their jobs. Tanya wanted Laura to take them in her home. Laura said she would take Matthew, but no one else. Tanya said to Laura, "Where Matthew goes, I go. If you won't take all three of us in, your grandson will be living in the car with us." So Laura took them in and had her son with his estranged wife, plus his wife's boyfriend! *The Hatfields and McCoys all together under the same roof!*

Some of Laura's in-laws were at Dad's house too. People constantly came and went, bringing food. Every time they went over to the mortuary, they ran into a constant stream of people coming in to pay their respects. There were so many flowers they had to move Dad out into the chapel the day before the funeral. The viewing room they had him in was too small to hold all of the flowers. Dad was very well known from having his own business for fifty years. After living in California for thirty years, Marty was amazed. People in California lived such a fast pace of life, it was a different world. Dad's living room was full of people when they were laughing and talking about how amazing it was that everyone else had aged! Then Laura said, "Everyone has aged but Marty, but the rest of us don't have all of her preservatives."

Byron, Brent, Faith and Marty left to go have dinner at the Harvest Inn. They were there three to four times everyday, even though they had food running out of their ears at Dad's house. Faith and Marty didn't want to eat at Dad's or even sit down to get contaminated. They were having a good time in the Harvest Inn when someone walked up to tell them how sorry they were to hear about Howard passing away. This happened many times when they were laughing and joking, like they were having a gay old time. Marty told Byron, "They probably think we are the most disrespectful kids they have ever seen. They have no idea how relieved we are that we don't have to worry about him anymore." Byron asked, "Do you think Laura will ever feel the relief we do?" Marty replied, "If she does, she wouldn't admit to anyone, not even herself."

Later that evening, Byron and Marty went over to Dad's house. They left Brent and Faith to have some time alone at the motel room, watching TV. No one else was in Dad's house but Delorse, Laura, Diana and Jenny. Jenny was Diana's sixteen year old daughter and she was a real cutie! Everyone else had retired for the evening in their campers parked by the alley in the backyard. Laura brought out all the family pictures she had found going through things. Howard's four kids spent the entire evening reminiscing with Diana and Jenny completely enthralled by it all. They laughed and talked for hours. Marty said to Jenny, "Your Grandma was a regular hellion when she was your age!" Laura said, "Marty! Don't say that to my sweet little granddaughter!" Laughing, Marty replied, "It's true! Remember when Dad took the car keys with him to work when he had his panel truck? You would hotwire the car and go anyway. Then he took off the distributor cap and you would just get another one off of one of the old cars in the back yard. Dad would drive through Larned late at night, going home from work, and here's Laura! You would be cruising down the main drag with a whole car load of kids!" Everyone cracked up.

When Byron and Marty left that night and got into the car, Marty turned to him and said, "This was a very special night; we will all remember this evening for the rest of our lives. Dad would have loved this, all of his kids sitting around laughing and having a good time. It's really a shame that he couldn't have been here." Byron said, "But he was here." Marty looked at him and said, "You know, I think you're right."

The next day, Byron and Marty stopped at the mortuary after breakfast before going to Dad's house. Brent and Faith were going shopping. The mortician told them one of the pallbearers called and couldn't make it, but he already had a replacement. Someone called the mortuary and asked to be one of the pallbearers. They asked who it was and he replied, "It was Arden Kobler from Hays." Byron and Marty said in unison, "No way!" Then Marty added, "Over my dead body!" The mortician just stood there befuddled and said, "What do you want me to do? I've already told him that we could use him." Marty answered, "You are going to call him back and tell him that you are sorry but the family already has a replacement. Actually, we really do. A very dear friend of Dad's just got home from vacation and we would love to have him as a pallbearer." The mortician said he would take care of it later. Marty said, "No you won't do it later. You are going to take care of it right now. I'm sorry we jumped on you so hard, but let me explain why. Arden Kobler is my ex-husband's brother. My present husband and I have been married for twenty-eight years! I don't know what it takes for these people to understand they are not part of this family!" The mortician said, "No wonder you're so upset! I understand and will call him right now!" Marty replied, "I would really appreciate it and while we are here, could you give me a copy of the invoice?" He said, "Oh, I don't want to bother you with that now." Marty replied, "Please bother me. I want to know the bottom line. I'm one of those nuts who like to know exactly where I am, at all times." Marty looked over the invoice and wrote out a check to him for half of it. She told him, "I'll mail you the balance after I get back to California in a few days." Marty noticed on the invoice they charged 1.5 percent on the unpaid balance each month. She hated spending money on interest, it was such a waste. Frank and Marty loved being debt free.

Laura saw to it that Dad had a funeral fit for a king; costing nearly six thousand dollars. Marty had made the comment to Frank when he was driving her to LAX, "They are going to have all of the arrangements made before I get there and I know Laura will go nuts!" She was right, the casket was the best they had to offer and the vault was as fancy as the casket. Frank and Marty knew for years that when the time came, they would be responsible for it all. They were the only ones who could afford it.

Byron and Marty left the mortuary and went over to Dad's. She showed the invoice to Laura and Diana. Laura had a fit when she saw the total. Marty wanted to ask her, "Didn't you ask about the costs at the time you were playing little rich bitch?" But she didn't; she kept her mouth shut, for now.

The funeral wasn't until Wednesday afternoon. They had a lovely room in the funeral home where the family greeted the guests as they arrived for the service. A few of Marty's old friends came to the service, driving twenty to seventy miles one way. The fact that they cared enough to come really touched her heart and it was so great to see them. Marty saw friends and cousins she had not seen for thirty to thirty-five years! Everyone looked so good to her even though they had to tell her who they were at first.

Marty was very busy greeting everyone when an elderly man walked up to her and smiled. She looked at him with a question in her eye. He asked, "You don't know who I am, do you?" She answered like she did a hundred times that week, "No, I am sorry, I don't." He said, "I'm Ray." Marty looked him right in the eye and asked, "Ray who?" He said, "Ray Kobler!" Oh my God! Marty was looking right at her ex-father-in-law and didn't have a clue! Then she saw his wife Charlotte and their son, Arden standing behind him. It never occurred to her when Arden wanted to be pallbearer that it was most likely they would be at the funeral. Charlotte told her, "Gib wanted to come so badly, but just couldn't get away. He is in Dallas now." Marty looked at her and said nothing, but she thought to herself, "Thank you, Lord!" Her ex-husband was the last person on earth she wanted to see there!

Marty glanced in the chapel and saw they had closed Dad's coffin. She freaked out and started to hyperventilate! Laura looked over and saw her. Marty said to Laura, "They closed the lid!" Laura came over and said, "Its okay, they will open it again later." Marty said, "No! No! You don't understand! Daddy can't breath!" Laura ran down the isle and told them they had to open the coffin again and leave it open. In a few minutes, she was okay. Shocked at her own reaction, Marty asked Faith, "Where did that come from? I know Dad isn't really there from all my religious beliefs!" Faith said, "Marty, this has nothing to do with your religious beliefs! This is your Daddy and you are having trouble letting go. It's perfectly normal."

John, one of Dad's buddies on his bowling team, walked up to Byron and Marty and said, "Do you know that your Dad is the third one of the five guys on our bowling team to die in the last three months?" Byron replied, "Look at it this way John, in two months you will all be bowling together in Heaven."

Aunt Lula's Baptist minister gave the service. Dad spent his entire life hopping from one church to another, looking for the perfect church. He just didn't understand that every church is made up of people and there was only one person who walked on earth who was perfect, Jesus. At the time Dad died, he was going to the Seventh Day Adventist Church. Aunt Lula said that minister would give the service over her dead body. As a result, the minister who did the service did not even know Dad personally, which was a real shame. Diana spent hours writing up a beautiful and loving eulogy for her grandpa, but didn't want to read it herself at the service. The preacher butchered it as he read it. It sounded like he didn't even bother to look at it before the service. Then he proceeded to tell a story about the cows using the same path, day after day, coming back to the barn from the pasture. He must have talked about his stupid cows for fifteen minutes to bring home a point, of how sorry he was that he had only crossed paths with Howard one time. After everyone was sick of hearing about these stupid cows, he said, "You are probably wondering what this has to do with Howard." Laura said loud enough for everyone in the family section to hear, "That's what I would like to know!" All of the kids and grandkids started snickering and had trouble regaining their composure!

After the graveside service, they had a buffet at Byron's house for close friends and family. Marty's friend Larry, a classmate and old boyfriend, came from out of town and they had a lovely visit. He knew where everyone was, what they were doing, and how many kids and grandkids everyone had.

The next day, the four kids went around town taking care of business. Everywhere they went all week, everyone knew Marty. She was getting embarrassed having to admit to everyone she did not know them, but they all knew her! Marty kept asking Laura and Byron, "How does everyone know who I am? I've changed a lot over the years." Finally, Laura and Byron said, "You really don't know, do you?" Marty answered, "No, I don't!" They both said, "It's because you are the only one in the family with any class! Look at you! You're dressed well, plus that mink coat with all your diamonds and rubies! What do you expect?" Marty replied, "It never occurred to me." She was just so overwhelmed to see all of those people that she didn't expect to ever see again.

They went to Dad's bank and Marty asked to speak with the manager. Three guys in suits came over to see her and Marty introduced herself. They quickly informed her that they already knew who she was and gave her their sincere condolences. The other kids hung back behind her as they had everywhere they went all day. It struck Marty more than a little funny, that as the baby of the family, she was taking care of business. She couldn't help remembering of years ago, when Dad and Laura treated her like she didn't have a brain in her head, even after she was on her own. Marty asked them, "Could you please check to see if Dad made a deposit last week? I sent him a check for five hundred dollars just a few days before he died, and no one has found it. They all spoke at once, "We don't have to check; we remember him coming in with it." Then one of them said he remembered vividly of Howard coming into the bank to deposit the check two days before he died. Your dad said to us, "Marty and Frank are always there whenever old Papa needs help. I don't even have to ask, they just know." Marty looked back over her shoulder at the other kids and said "Well, at least now we know what happened to it." When she looked back, Byron was grinning from ear to ear looking at Laura out of the corner of his eye. She looked over at Laura and steam was coming out of both ears! Marty thought to herself, "Well now you know, sister dear, that you were not the only one who helped Dad!" Marty gave them her phone number in case they needed more funds. She had no idea how many checks Dad had written or if there were funds to cover them. They started to walk out of the bank when someone said, "Marty!" Marty turned around and one of her high school friends, Marion, was working there. After chatting a bit, she started out of the bank again when someone from the other side of the bank said, "Marty!" She turned around and another one of her high school friends, Karen, was working there too and they chatted for a few minutes. Who said you can't go home again! It was so great seeing everyone!

While they were running all over town, they ran into one of their cousins, Dr. Earl. He was delivering a baby the day before and couldn't make it to the funeral. Dr. Earl's dad, Uncle Cecil, was the only one left of that entire generation on their mama's side and he was at the funeral. Dr. Earl told them about calling his dad to let him know that Uncle Howard was gone and said that his dad didn't say anything for a full minute, and then stated, "That's not possible! I just saw Howard a few days ago." Marty said, "I knew it was going to be difficult for your dad. They were buddies long before they met the two sisters." Dr. Earl smiled and said to Marty, "It's funny you brought that up because that was the next thing Dad said to me, "Howard was my brother before he was my brother-in-law."

Uncle Cecil and Dad were best buddies throughout school. Several years after Dad left home, Uncle Cecil and Aunt Ifa met and were getting married. Dad was Uncle Cecil's Best Man and Mama was her sister's Maid of Honor. After the wedding and reception, no one could find Howard or Merab. They really hit it off and left the premises! It was about one year later, they were married too!

Dr. Earl's wife, Kathy was with him. Delorse said to Kathy, "Oh, I remember you. You're one of the twins!" The rest of the kids said, "No Delorse, Kathy is not the twin." Kathy spoke up and said, "You're right, I'm the second wife. But we've been married for seventeen years; doesn't that count for something?" Marty replied, "Its okay Kathy, I'm on my second marriage too and we've been married for twenty-eight years." Dr. Earl spoke up and said to Laura, "You will have to apologize to your husband, Estel, for me. We went over to Uncle Howard's looking for you all and Estel was out in the yard by one of the old cars. It took him thirty minutes to convince me that he belonged there. I tried to run him off the place because I thought he was a bum." Marty and Byron looked at each other and almost lost it. They wanted to crack up! Laura looked at Dr. Earl and said, "I guess you know that I am the only one of us kids who's still with their original spouse." Byron piped up and said sarcastically, "That's only because you haven't got the guts to get a divorce!" Marty wanted to applaud Byron! She looked at Dr. Earl instead and he gave her a big smile.

Marty had heard that statement from Laura a hundred times and wanted to scream bloody murder every time! In the first place, she was completely discounting the fact that Byron was not divorced! His wife was killed in the car accident with his little girl. In the second place, Laura's marriage was a sick joke! Her husband was a complete bastard! Now Laura's son, Roy, talks exactly like his dad. Roy wasn't able to go to the funeral because he had the flu. Byron and Marty were counting their blessings because they didn't know how Roy would come dressed for the funeral. At least Estel wore a suit and they were shocked that he even had one. Delorse's son-in-law said to Marty later, "Roy had the flu my ass, he had the DDT's; I was in the Navy and have seen it enough to know. Didn't you think it was very strange, Aunt Marty, that no one else in the entire family caught the flu from him?" Marty said, "I never gave it a thought!"

After they ran all over town taking care of business, Marty asked if they could go out to the cemetery. The four children stood together by Dad and Mom in their graves. Marty thought, "Dad and Mom are finally together again after fifty-one years." It was very strange, but it was like they had come to a complete circle. Marty felt more at peace than she had ever felt in her life.

They went back to Byron's house and said their good-byes. This was probably the last time all four kids would be together in this lifetime. Marty honestly hated to leave, but Brent, Faith, and Marty had to get on the road to Kansas City. Marty was flying back to California the next morning.

After driving for three hours, they stopped at a coffee shop to eat. By then, they were so exhausted that they acted like they had three drinks too many. *When they were driving to Larned from Kansas City four days before, they ate at the same coffee shop and had ordered pie for dessert, but it never came. When Marty paid the check, she told the cashier, and she removed it from the ticket.* This time, Faith noticed the comment cards and filled one out.

They cracked up as she wrote, "We ordered pie four days ago and we are still waiting for it." Then they noticed two highway patrolmen across the room, who were watching them. Marty said, "Don't be surprised if they pull us over after we get back on the road, to see if we are sober!"

Dad had passed away just two weeks after the Oklahoma City bombing. They drove right through Junction City where the FBI found the second Ryder truck in the lake. The bombers had rented three Ryder trucks and had only used one in the bombing. The FBI had not been able to locate the third one. Brent kept saying to Faith and Marty, "Just let me know if you see a Ryder truck so I can keep my distance!"

It was late and there was a lot of fog as they approached Topeka. The fog was really thick, but everyone on the interstate was still going seventy miles an hour. Marty said to Brent when they were almost to Lawrence, "This is really stupid Brent. If we got a motel room in Lawrence, how long would it take us to get to the airport from there?" Brent answered, "It would only be forty-five minutes." Marty said, "Let's pull off and get a room. Brent asked, "Do you want to stay at the Holiday Inn? It's pretty nice and that's where Dad always stayed when I was in college here." Marty said, "Sure, it will be fine." When they pulled into the Holiday Inn, Faith was asleep. Brent and Marty went into the office to check in and didn't wake her. Marty asked the guy at the desk, "You do know there is a Ryder truck parked out there, right? He smiled and said yes. Marty then asked, "You have had it checked out, right?" Just as she was asking, Faith walked in and said, "Aunt Marty! You don't joke about things like that!" Marty said, "Faith, I'm not joking! There really is a Ryder truck parked out there!"

The Holiday Inn in Lawrence was really big, with the Kansas University there. They drove to their room and an FBI vehicle, with FBI shirts hanging up in it, was parked next to them. It was certainly not something you would ever expect to see in Kansas!

They pulled into the Kansas City International Airport only fifteen minutes before the time of departure for Marty's flight. She grabbed her bags and ran in out of breath. The check-in agent told her to slow down and take a breath. The plane she was taking had not even landed yet because of the fog.

Marty said her farewells to Brent and Faith, telling them they didn't need to wait with her. She said, "You are both so tired, go home and get some rest." Faith said to her "I really expected this week to be a real downer, under the circumstances. Thanks to you, I had more fun this week than I've had in my life! I've never bonded to anyone as easily as I did with you. You are a very special person, and I'm proud to have you as my aunt." Marty told them both, "It was no accident that the two of you met and fell in love. Its God's plan! You are perfect for each other! I wish you both all the happiness in the world!"

Marty just barely made her connecting flight in Houston because of the delay in Kansas City. When she landed in LAX, the air quality was perfectly clear with no smog, and it was beautiful. When she stepped off the plane, Frank was waiting for her with a big smile, and Toby showered Mom with his kisses when they got to the car. When they got home, it looked like a mansion to her! Marty was once again in her safe haven with Frank and little Toby.

CHAPTER FORTY-FOUR

There wasn't time to get unpacked before the phone started ringing and it was either Byron or Laura. Byron started complaining that Laura was walking off with everything of value—Dad's antique furniture, clocks, and guns. He had one antique gun that was worth a bloody fortune. It was a cap and ball musket used to fight Indians in Kentucky by Marty's great, great grandfather. In fact, Marty's great grandmother was an Indian squaw who died in childbirth when grandpa was born, but no one knew what tribe she was from. Marty's grandpa refused to talk about it. He didn't know it was something to be proud of; being a real native red blooded American.

Byron told Marty people were hounding him to death about Dad's bills. Marty sent him the money to pay all of them in full, to take the pressure off of him. Two weeks after Marty sent him the money, he still hadn't paid the bills. He said he didn't have time. So Marty called him at 10:00 a.m. on his day off and said, "This is your wake up call to go pay bills today!" He answered very begrudgingly, "Thanks a lot!" Frank and Marty shelled out over twelve thousand dollars for the bills plus other expenses. The funeral, hospital, doctors, material used on his jobs, a small outstanding loan, utilities and miscellaneous bills were all paid in full.

Two weeks later, Laura and her family went back to Kansas, to clean out more crap and loaded up with more antique furniture to take back to Colorado. While they were there, Delorse pulled up with a U-Haul trailer with her daughter-in-law from Texas. She parked in front on the street and Laura's vehicles were parked in the back yard. Delorse got the surprise of her life when she walked into the house and saw Laura. She didn't expect anyone to be there. Byron told Marty on the phone, "When Laura and her family pulled out in their five wheeler and other vehicles; they didn't have room for a pack of cigarettes." He got tired of seeing everyone else take things, so Byron jumped in and took things he didn't even want. Marty laughed and told Frank, "They are just like a bunch of stray alley cats fighting over table scraps thrown out behind a diner." Laura kept asking Marty what she wanted and she kept telling Laura she didn't want anything. She wanted to say, "What on earth makes you think I would want any of that crap? I wouldn't want to contaminate my house!" Marty couldn't get past the fact, the furniture and everything else in Dad's house had mice running around in it and on it. She didn't understand why that fact didn't bother the rest of them. She asked Frank, "How in the hell can I be related to these people? Cleanliness doesn't seem to be in their vocabulary!"

It reminded her of the last time Dad was in California. He told her, "When the time comes, I want you to know who to hire for the auctioneer." Marty told him, "Dad, there won't be any auction. Laura will arrive with a big semi-truck and haul it all back to Colorado." Dad was horrified that she would say such a thing and said, "Your sister wouldn't do that!" Marty looked up to the sky and said, "Hey Dad! Do you see your perfect little Laura now?"

Marty really felt that Laura and her kids well deserved to have some of the things they took because they worked their butts off clearing all the crap out of the house and getting rid of the old cars. They had to go through stacks and stacks of newspapers, magazines, and junk mail. It was in those stacks that they found the deeds to his houses, titles for many of his old cars and other important papers. They really earned every bit of what they took; the job they did was a nightmare. What was hard for Marty to swallow is how Laura played down the value of everything they took. She said none of it had much value; they just wanted the things out of *sentiment*. Laura went on and on, telling Marty about all the things that were promised to her and her kids. Everything that had significant value, Dad promised to Laura and her family. Then Marty found out that Laura's son, Roy, had sold the van he got from his grandpa, after he fixed it up. She wondered how many other things they sold that they had taken *for sentiment*. Finally Marty said to Laura on the phone, "When you are dissolving an estate where there's a problem of bringing in enough money to pay the bills, it doesn't matter a damn what was promised to whom!"

By the time everything was sold and settled, Marty was only out two thousand dollars of expenses she did not turn in to the attorney. No one else turned in expenses either. After the attorney was paid, each child received four hundred dollars. Marty gave her four hundred to Byron. She also bought him a nice set of luggage and mailed him an airline ticket to come to California. After he arrived, Frank and Marty took him to Las Vegas and paid for everything to celebrate! The estate was settled! They stayed at the Mirage and dined at lovely places.

Marty was always trying to make up for the hard time Byron had in life. Frank saw him as being lazy, with no ambition; a person who didn't do anything to help himself. Marty found herself constantly defending Byron to Frank, telling him he didn't know what Byron had been through, with Dad and Laura constantly on his ass. Then he lost his wife and little girl. Marty took it upon herself to try and make up for it. She was her brother's keeper.

CHAPTER FORTY-FIVE

Toby had surgery to remove a tumor from his little hip and it affected his kidneys. He never bounced back from the surgery and went down hill very fast. Marty could see it in his eyes that he was suffering. The small bits of aspirin she gave him didn't help. She held him for hours and rocked him.

Frank had always made jokes that Toby thought Mom could fix anything. He would only take medication from Mom and only wanted his Mom when he didn't feel good. Toward the end when Marty was holding and rocking him, he looked up at her and gave her that look that said, "Mommy fix." Marty gave him kisses with the tears streaming down her face and said, "Mommy can't fix this one baby." He was only three months away from his fourteenth birthday. One day Toby had a really bad time of it and when Frank came home from work Marty told him, "I think it's time. We can't let Toby go on suffering like this." They spent the entire evening showering him with love and attention. The next morning Frank said his final good-by to Toby and left for work. Later that morning, Marty took him down to the vet. She cradled him in her arms telling him over and over, "Mommy loves you," while they gave him the shot with tears streaming down her face. She just barely made it back to the car before completely losing it. It was even more difficult than when they lost Buttons and she didn't know that was possible. Toby's little heart was filled with nothing but love; he had been the joy of their lives.

When Frank came home that night, he said, "Toby is in Heaven now having ice cream with his grandpa." When Marty's dad came to visit them every year, Grandpa and Toby had ice cream together every night at bedtime. Grandpa worshipped the ground Toby walked on and would jump when Toby wanted something. Marty had not seen her Dad do that for anyone in her life! When they took Dad to the airport every year for his flight home, the tears rolled down Toby's little cheeks. The first time it happened, Dad was so touched he was almost speechless. He said, "I didn't know puppy dogs could actually cry." Marty answered, "Toby doesn't know he's a dog, Dad. I think that's why he loves little kids. He thinks he's one of them."

Frank and Marty were surprised and very touched by the number of sympathy cards they received for their loss from friends and neighbors. Marty was a basket case. She kept seeing a vision in her mind of Toby running around Heaven saying, "This is really great, but where's my Mom, I need my Mom."

CHAPTER FORTY-SIX

One Saturday, Frank walked into the house with total strangers. Marty thought he had lost his mind inviting strangers into their home. A realtor had taken them to the house next door because she thought they were interested in selling their home. The neighbor only wanted an appraisal. Frank was in the front yard weeding. After the realtor left, Tom and Linda came over to Frank and introduced themselves. They commented on how much they liked his house and location. Frank offered to show them the inside. The couple seemed to be very nice people and gave Marty their business cards plus their home phone number. They said, "We would really appreciate it if you could call us when a house like yours goes up for sale in this neighborhood. It is exactly what we want and we love what you have done with it." Marty took the cards and said she would be happy to call them. She really liked Tom and Linda and thought they would make great neighbors.

Frank came home one day and said, "This project I'm on is nearly completed and I have to find another project to get on or be out of a job again." He worked hard to find another position within the company. Finally, they told him the only position they had open was in the Pasadena office for twelve small projects. His title was still *Principle Project Control Engineer*, but he was now reporting to twelve different Project Managers. The job required a lot of walking, going to offices on different floors for meetings and collecting data for his reports. His bad leg was taking a beating, and he told his boss after a couple of weeks that he could not be on his bad leg that much; he couldn't take the pain. His boss promised they would find something else for him the following week. Every week, it was *next week*. After this went on for over four months, he came home one day and could barely walk. Marty said, "This is it, Frank! You are going to call in sick tomorrow and I'm taking you to the doctor." His knee was killing him and it was so swollen it was difficult for him to remove his dress pants.

The next day, Marty got him in to see an orthopedic surgeon. Dr. Bittner didn't know how he could possibly walk. They ran tests, took x-rays, and scheduled surgery. The surgery went well, but his knee was full of arthritis. Dr. Bittner said he would need a knee replacement in four to five years when he reached the point he could no longer take the pain. Frank had to go through extensive physical therapy and used crutches to get around. Frank and Marty thought after he recuperated that he would be back to where he was with his bad leg before the last position at Ralph M. Parsons. They were wrong; his leg would never be that mobile again. Then after the bastards at Ralph M. Parsons almost destroyed his leg, they informed him that when he recuperated from the surgery he would no longer have a job. Marty could see that Frank couldn't work on that leg any longer and made a suggestion, "If we move to a less expensive area to live and buy a smaller house, you could retire now." Frank replied, "No way!"

Marty got on the computer and made the changes in their retirement charts. The charts had all of their accounts with average percentages of interest every year for growth; their income less expenses with cost of living increases each year on the expenses allowing for inflation; plus figuring what the federal and state taxes would be every year. She put in extra expenses for the years they plan to buy a car and also for upkeep and decorating the house. The charts covered the next twenty-five years. She updated her budget every month and the charts at least once a year. There was no doubt about it, they could move and retire now with no problem! Frank couldn't believe it!

They looked at several retirement communities in Southern California and were not crazy about any of them. Marty thought of a friend of hers that bought a house in a retirement community in Las Vegas. They bought the house for a place to stay when they went to Las Vegas every two to four weeks. Marty's friend had passed away two weeks after her Dad died. Marty called her husband and he gave her all the information and told her, "You will love it!" Then she called "Del Webb Sun City Summerlin" and made reservations for their "try before you buy program." They went to Las Vegas three to four times a year and were already confident that they would love living there.

A few days before Frank and Marty were to leave for Las Vegas and check it out; Marty said to Frank, "I'm going to give Tom and Linda a call to see if they have found a house yet. Frank asked, "Who are you talking about?" She answered, "The couple you brought into our house after they looked at the house next door." Frank said, "Don't be ridiculous. It's probably been six months since they were here. They have bought and moved by now." Marty replied, "It won't cost a thing to call and find out." It was a Saturday morning, so Marty called their home phone number they had given her. She still had their business cards. Usually, she threw out everything she didn't need any more. She cleaned out that drawer two or three times in the past few months and almost threw the cards out each time, but her little voice kept telling her not to do it. Marty was a firm believer in listening to her little voice.

Linda answered the phone and Marty explained, "Linda, you probably don't remember me, but this is Marty Wurtz. You and Tom were in Yorba Linda Hills several months ago looking for a house and gave me your business cards. If you are still interested, I wanted to let you know that we are selling our house." Linda exploded with excitement! She said, "Of course I remember you! I would never forget your house! You will never believe this, but just this morning at the breakfast table I told Tom, 'We have looked in every inch of Yorba Linda Hills and the only house we have seen that I want is Marty and Frank's and they are not going anywhere.'" They came over that day and when they arrived, Marty showed them through the house again. She poured everyone a drink; then they all sat down in the living room and talked turkey. Marty explained about Frank's surgery and the need for them to move so he could retire early. Frank said, "Nothing is written in stone yet, but we are going to Sun City in Las Vegas next week to check it out. We'll give you a call when we get home."

Frank's Dad and Mary came down the next day. Frank and Marty explained to them what they were doing and why. They were not happy, to say the very least, but Dad asked if they could hitch a ride with them to a hotel at State Line. They had a special rate for staying there and Dad loved all the cheap deals. All the way to State Line, Dad kept telling Frank, "Don't do anything stupid." It was the last thing he said when they dropped them off at their hotel.

Frank and Marty arrived in Las Vegas and found "Del Webb Sun City Summerlin" by the Spring Mountain Range at one of the highest points in the Las Vegas Valley! It was beautiful and they fell in love with the place! The community centers were lovely, and the golf course by the sales office had ponds with water falls, ducks and geese. There were three golf courses in Sun City. They checked into their villa which had a lovely view of the Las Vegas Valley. The next day, they went through all fourteen models and Marty fell in love with the Warwick. Frank questioned her, "Are you sure you can be happy in a house this small?" It was twelve hundred and thirty square feet. Marty replied, "This is exactly what I want, I'm retiring too! I don't want to slave on a house until I drop dead!" It had everything Marty wanted and nothing that she didn't want—the floor plan was perfect!

They had an appointment with a saleswoman, Charlene. Marty told her, "We have already looked at all the models and we want a Warwick." Charlene commented, "You and everyone else! That is our most popular model." She pointed out the Warwicks on the map around the perimeter of Sun City that were still available. Marty said, "No, we want on the golf course.

Charlene said, "We have one Warwick left on the golf course, but its forty thousand dollars over the base price for the view." Frank and Marty answered at the same time, "We don't care, that's the one we want!" Charlene ran down the hall to put a hold on it. Then she took them up to the lot to show them the location. The house was not built yet, but the golf course was there and behind the golf course was the Spring Mountain Range. The view was incredible! In front of the house, they would have a partial view of the city lights. This was it! This was where they were going to spend the rest of their days with beautiful blue skies and fluffy white clouds! They thought they had died and gone to Heaven! Frank asked Charlene to hold the house for one day so they could sleep on it. The next day, they saw Charlene again to sign all the papers and gave her a deposit of five thousand dollars.

At one point, Marty excused herself to go outside in front of the sales office to have a cigarette. She saw a familiar car driving up to the entrance; Nancy and Marty said at the same time, "Oh my God! Is that you?" Nancy and her husband, Tom, played Bridge with Frank and Marty for nearly twenty years. Of all their friends, Tom and Nancy were two of their favorites. Nancy's parents, Shirley and Bert, moved in across the street from Frank and Marty years ago when they lived in the townhouse. Shirley was also in the ladies bridge groups. Nancy and Tom were in the process of moving to Las Vegas too. Shirley came up with Nancy and they decided to come over to check out where Frank and Marty wanted to buy. They were cracking up. What were the odds of Marty standing out there at the precise moment they drove by, but what the heck, this is Vegas! Nancy asked, "Are you going to do it?" Marty answered, "Frank is in there signing our life away as we speak!" Nancy was thrilled!

The next day, Frank and Marty took a bus tour of the area provided by Del Webb, their builder. They met a fun couple on the tour who were going to be their neighbors, Ken and Betty. After the tour, they spent five hours in the design center. They had their choice of a hundred different options, plus picked out carpet, tile, and shutters. It was unbelievable the number of options they had to offer, for a price. Ken and Betty had already been through that and came in to the design center to see how they were doing. Ken asked, "Has she asked yet if you want indoor plumbing?" Everyone thought it was hysterical except the designer. She gave Ken a mischievous dirty look.

When they were finished with all the decisions, they walked out completely drained. Marty asked Frank, "Do you realize we haven't even been down to the strip yet? They had been so busy, they hadn't even thought about it. This was their last night before going home, so they went down to the Mirage for dinner and to gamble a while on the nickel slots. Marty didn't want to go home; she just wanted to stay there. In a few months, though, this would be home.

The next day, they picked up Dad and Mary at State Line. They met them in the coffee shop of their hotel to have breakfast. After they chatted for a few minutes, Marty said, "Well, we did it! We bought a duplex in Sun City!" They were royally pissed! Dad said, "I thought I told you not to do anything stupid!" Frank said to Marty later, "I should have come right back and said it was the smartest thing I've ever done to get away from my loving family who don't even want to see us on Thanksgiving!"

Frank was over fifty-six years old and his Dad was still trying to run his life. It didn't matter to Dad that they were making this move so Frank could get off his leg and retire. They would get fifty percent more out of the California house than they were putting into the house in Las Vegas, including all of the upgrades and the cost of the view. Nevada had no state income tax. Their property taxes would be half of what they were in California. The cost of living was less in Nevada than California. The dry climate would be much better for Frank's leg and Marty's back with a lot less humidity than California. They would have things to do they both enjoyed and were able to do with their physical limitations. Traveling was difficult for both of them. It was not easy for Frank to get around and Marty couldn't sit or stand for long periods of time.

When Frank and Marty were looking for a retirement community in Southern California, Marty looked at the map for the location of each one to see how long it would take them to get to Las Vegas from that point. Marty mentioned this to friends, so after they bought their new house in Sun City; their friends asked, "Do you think you got close enough to Vegas?" Twenty years ago, Marty never wanted to go to Vegas again after seeing the man shot in the Aladdin, now she was going to live there!

Marty called Linda when they got home and said, "We did it! We bought a house in Las Vegas!" Linda was ecstatic! She said, "We knew you would." They contacted an escrow company and set up a date to sign the papers; then the four of them went out to dinner to celebrate!

Frank and Marty told all of their neighbors and friends, "We have retired, sold our house and moving to Vegas!" They all went into shock! The neighbors asked, "What do you mean you have sold your house? You haven't even had a sign up. Where did you find the buyers?" Frank and Marty replied, "They came to our front door!"

Tom and Linda sold their house and had to move by the end of September. Frank and Marty's house in Las Vegas wouldn't be completed until the end of December. So they rented a small house in Sun City for three months on the telephone, sight unseen. Marty had to do all the packing because Frank couldn't do much with his knee and leg. He was still going five days a week for extensive therapy.

Marge had a family dinner for them just before they left. The reception Frank and Marty received was cold as ice! Marty invited everyone to come to Vegas to see them, but when she asked Melody and Terri, they just gave her a look that said, "Yeah, right." Their mother Marge had done a real number on them. The difficult good-byes they had were all of their friends.

Moving day arrived and they were off to Las Vegas! When Frank stopped at the first stop light in Vegas, there was a very loud clunk. The transmission dropped. Frank just kept going very slowly. They arrived just in time to pick up their keys at the

real estate office for the rental before they closed for the day.
When they walked into their rental, the place was filthy! Frank
took one look at the kitchen and said, "We're not cooking here.
We'll eat out every night." They stayed at a local hotel the first
night, not far from Sun City, but they needed to unload all of
the valuables out of the car before leaving it unattended at the
hotel. The carpet was covered with dead bugs and dust. So they
dug the vacuum out of the car and vacuumed the place before
unloading. The hotel room left a lot to be desired. Marty laughed
and said, "Well, it certainly isn't the Mirage!" Their furniture and
everything else arrived in perfect condition the next day. Marty
called the real estate office and demanded they send someone
over to clean the place. The manager came over himself and he
did a good job, not to Marty's standards, but okay. After he left,
Marty cleaned everything again and she cleaned the toilets six
times before she could handle using them. They laughed and
just kept reminding each other, "It's just for three months! We
can do this! We are survivors!"

Frank drove the car to the Chrysler dealer for a new
transmission, praying all the way that it would get him there.
He rented a car while their car was in the shop. They had sold
Frank's little Honda a few weeks before moving, after Marty
pointed out how much they would save by not having the
expense of a second car.

Two days after arriving, Frank and Marty went to the sales
office to see Charlene. As soon as she saw them she asked,
"Have you been up to your lot yet?" They laughed and said, "No,
we would never be able to find it." Charlene grabbed her car
keys and said, "Let's go!" The slab had been poured and the fire
wall was up between the two dwellings, but that was it. They
couldn't believe their house would be complete in three months.
Charlene assured them that it would be completed by the end
of December.

They didn't unpack anymore than they had to at the rental.
It was just a place to sleep and spend as little time at as possible.
They went out to eat all the time. Everyday they went up to see
the progress on their new house. Many friends wanted to come

to Las Vegas to see them. Marty told everyone, "Not until we are in our house. We wouldn't want the devil himself to see our hell-hole rental."

Two months after moving to Las Vegas, they celebrated their thirtieth wedding anniversary at Kokomos in the Mirage. Marty asked, "Can you imagine what our reaction would have been if someone had told us when we were here celebrating our twenty-fifth anniversary that we would be retired in five years and living here in Las Vegas?" Frank replied, "I would have said there was no way, I'll only be fifty-six years old!" When their waiter asked where they moved from after they mentioned that they were locals, he said that he had an aunt who lived in Yorba Linda, CA. It turned out that Marty played bridge with his Aunt Jean for many years!

The Mirage will always have a very special place in their hearts, but they started discovering other lovely places. They dined on top of the Stratosphere where they viewed the incredible lights of the entire Las Vegas Valley. The Voo Doo Café on top of the Rio has a gorgeous view of the lights on the strip. Las Vegas is the adult Disneyland of the world!

The day after Christmas, they moved into their new house and it was wonderful just to kiss their hell-hole rental good-bye. Everything looked beautiful. The quality of the construction was better than any house they ever had in California. They just barely got settled and people started coming up to Vegas to see them. Dad and Mary were the first; they loved their house and Sun City. Dad even said if they were ten years younger, they would move next door. (God forbid!) During the first year in Vegas, they had nineteen visits from friends and family. Everyone stayed at a hotel, but Frank and Marty drove them all over town and took them to the nicest places to dine. Dad and Mary came up every couple of months. Marge and Dick came up twice a year. Many friends came up and they had a ball!

They made many new friends and saw a lot of Ken and Betty, their new neighbors they met when they came up to buy their house. John and Ellen, who moved in down the street are a fun couple from New York. They are an absolute riot! Natural born comedians! The whole neighborhood has really nice and friendly people. Everyone looks out for each other. Frank and Marty had no idea retirement would be this great! Beautiful new hotel casinos dripping in elegance started popping up on the strip plus lovely new local hotel casinos around different parts of the valley: The Bellagio, Venetian, Mandalay Bay, the new Aladdin, Paris Las Vegas, Palms Casino Resort, Green Valley Ranch, Suncoast, the Resort at Summerlin that is now the Rampart and J.W. Marriott Hotel, and other new local places.

Frank was still having a lot of pain and problems with his knee and leg, but he kept going to the gym to do his therapy exercises religiously. He bought a cane and that helped him get around. Everyone who came to Vegas for a visit understood that Frank could not do a lot of walking; everyone but his family. After Frank's family left each time, Frank was in excruciating pain and Marty's legs were killing her.

They spent four to six hours on the phone every Sunday, talking to Frank's Dad, Marge, Laura and Byron. Marty's sister and brother would get on the phone and talk about absolutely nothing between two and three hours each! It would take six tries to get off the phone. Marty's ears, head, and neck would kill her by the time she got off the phone every Sunday. She had to have a back treatment every Monday.

It didn't matter if Frank and Marty had friends visiting from out of state; precisely at 7:00 p.m. every Sunday night, Frank had to call his Dad. One night they were late getting home and called Dad at 8:00 p.m. Dad went into a tail spin and said he was ready to call 911. He acted like they had committed an unforgivable mortal sin!

It was certainly no surprise, but when Marge and Dick came to Las Vegas, they had no consideration whatsoever for Frank and Marty's physical limitations! One night during dinner, Marty told Marge her legs were killing her and she didn't think she could go party with them that night. Marge never said a word. She just gave Marty her catty little smile that said one of two things; "I don't believe you or I don't care if you are hurting, you are going whether you like it or not!" Marty went and when they dropped them off late that night, Marge and Dick announced, "We'll pick you up at your house at seven a.m. to go to breakfast." Marty answered, "I am not getting up at six a.m. just to go to breakfast." Marge repeated herself, "We will be at your house at seven a.m. Be ready to go to breakfast!" The next morning, Frank met them at the front door. He told them, "Marty's still in bed asleep and you are not going to disturb her! Her legs are still killing her!"

Dad and Mary always came up to Las Vegas on senior citizen bus tours. After a few years, they suddenly quit coming and took the bus tours to Laughlin. Frank and Marty would drive down to Laughlin for the day to see them. Dad kept protesting saying it was too far for them to come just for the day. It was a two hour drive one way. Dad quit letting Frank pay for their dinners. When they came to Vegas, Frank and Marty took them to the nicest buffets in town and picked up the tab. Dad only wanted to go to buffets.

Frank had gone to California to visit several times the first two years and stayed at a motel. After two years when Frank told his Dad on the phone that he was coming to California, his Dad's reply would be, "Why?" Frank would answer, "To visit family and friends." Dad would then ask, "What for?" This happened three different times and each time Frank would say to Marty, "If that's his attitude, then why should I go?" Marty knew that Frank felt like his Dad had kicked him right in the gut. He didn't care about seeing his only son.

Frank and Marty still went to Laughlin to see them every time Dad and Mary went there on their senior citizen bus tours. Dad kept protesting, saying it was too far for them to come. Then Dotty, Frank's cousin called one night and mentioned the fact that Dad and Mary just got back from Laughlin. Dad had not said a word on the phone about it. Frank called his Dad and told him, "I want to know when you go to Laughlin." Frank and Marty went down to see them when they went again a couple of mouths later.

Dad told Frank that he was leaving money to his two granddaughters and two great grandsons. The sixty thousand dollars were coming out of Frank's share, not Marge's. Frank said, "No problem." Then the next time they saw Dad and Mary, Dad said he was leaving his condo worth over two hundred and fifty thousand dollars to Marge. Frank told his Dad again, "No problem."

The next time Frank went alone to Laughlin because Marty's back and legs were killing her. Marty didn't want Frank to go that day because they predicted very strong winds on the weather forecast. In the middle of the open desert is the last place you want to be with high winds and there's absolutely nothing between Las Vegas and Laughlin. Frank would not tell his Dad he couldn't come because of high winds; that would sound like a cop out. Frank would have gone if he had to crawl there through the damn desert to see his father! Even after his Dad protested his coming, saying that it was too far! Frank still thought he had to go! If his Dad ever asked him to kiss his bare ass, Frank would have done that too, with a smile on his face!

Marty spent the day watching TV, seeing all the reports on the wind. They showed truck drivers on the freeway in the middle of Las Vegas who said they couldn't see five feet in front of their face. Marty couldn't stand it another minute and called Dad's hotel room in Laughlin. She lucked out; they were in the room and she asked to speak to Frank. He was totally unaware of the weather reports and said the wind wasn't blowing there. Marty said to him, "If you want to come home today, you better get your ass on the road now!" It took Frank four and a half hours to get home which was normally a two hour drive. He was detoured over to California at a road block because the visibility was zero between there and Las Vegas. By the time he got home, Marty didn't know whether to give him a hug or kill him! She had been a nervous wreck, worrying about him the entire day!

Frank sat down and told her the latest news flash, "Dad told me he is leaving even more to Marge. As usual, he purposely waited for my car to come up at valet when I was leaving before telling me, so I didn't have a chance to say two words about it. I thought about it all the way home. He is leaving the bulk of his entire estate to Marge, Melody, Terri, and Terri's kids. He said I will get one hundred and thirty thousand dollars." Marty asked, "When are you going to wake up Frank? Don't you see what's going on here? He's working up to cutting you out completely. That's why he quit letting us pick up the tabs, quit coming to Las Vegas and didn't want us to go out of our way to come to Laughlin or California. It's also why he's telling you what he is doing; his guilty conscience is working on him. That's why Marge and Dick didn't let you pay for dinner the last two times they were here. They didn't want to be obligated to you. Where is your pride? Beat him to the punch. Call your Dad when he gets home and suggest that he leave it all to Marge and be done with it. Your sweet sister has been working on him all of her life. Every time she needed anything over the years, she played broke to her Daddy and he bought it for her. The last time I went to Laughlin with you, he was talking about poor Marge and how she struggled. Then he told us they bought a new second car and paid thirty-six thousand dollars for it. I said to Dad, 'They paid thirty-six thousand dollars for a second car? We don't even have a second car and we didn't pay that for our only car!' Dad said he never gave that a thought." Frank said to Marty, "You used to fall for Marge's stories just like Dad. Remember the time Marge cried to you that their TV wasn't working and they couldn't afford to fix it or get a new one. You wanted to take our portable Sony color TV that was in our bedroom up to them, saying we never used it anyway. It was like new. I didn't want to do it, but you felt so sorry for Marge. We went up there for a family dinner and after I brought it in, Dick proudly brought out a lens he just bought for his camera for five hundred dollars! I wanted to pick the TV up and put it back in the car!"

Frank didn't go to bed that night until 4:00 a.m. He spent hours sitting at the dining room table writing down everything he wanted to say to Marge. He called her soon after he got up that morning and let it all hang out. Then he summed it all up by saying, "I am sick and tired of you lying to Dad, your constant manipulating him and conniving to get everything and anything you want and to hell with me. You no longer have a brother. I don't ever want to hear from you or see you again." Marge's only reply was, "It sounds like you have really thought a lot about this." Frank was amazed at her response! She didn't even try to deny anything! After Frank hung up Marty said to him, "I am really proud of you; you never once raised your voice and didn't use any foul language." Frank called his Dad that night and was very friendly, telling him about the detour he had when driving home from Laughlin in the wind. Dad was not talking. Then Frank said in a nice and calm manner, "Dad, I've been thinking about what you said, concerning your estate. I really don't think what you are doing is fair." Dad exploded and started yelling, "Who in the hell do you think you are, telling me what to do with my money? What are you going to do about it, sue me?" Frank answered calmly, "No, I would not sue you. You know I'm not cut out that way. Why don't you just leave it all to Marge and be done with it? Dad started yelling again, "This is Marty talking, not you!" Frank answered in a firm manner, "You leave Marty out of this. This is between you and me." Dad then said sarcastically, "You can tell Marty she can get off the phone now." Frank remained calm, but firm and said, "She is not on the phone. She's standing in the kitchen rubbing blue ice on her legs because they are still killing her. I can see her from where I'm sitting in the living room." Dad said abruptly, "I don't want to talk anymore," and hung up.

Frank's cousin, Dottie, called later and told them about the nuclear fall out in California. Marge had called Dad and fed him full of lies, as usual. She said Frank had yelled and screamed at her, calling her a whore and a slut.

The following Sunday, Frank called his Dad at the normal time. Frank did not bring up anything about the will or Marge. He was just making small talk. After a couple of minutes Dad said, "This is awkward; I don't want to talk anymore." He hung up. The next Sunday, Frank called his Dad again. The same thing happened; Dad did not want to talk and hung up. Frank didn't call again. He told Marty, "He doesn't have to beat me over the head, if he doesn't want to talk, I won't call." Frank was really hurting. He had been a model son to the bastard for sixty-one years and he just got shit in the face for it.

However, his eyes were suddenly wide open! Marty didn't think that would happen in Frank's lifetime. He spent his life with blinders on when it came to his Dad. There were times that Frank acted like his Dad was God. Marty never understood what Frank saw in his Dad that made him act as if he was in awe of him. Dad was very rude and belligerent to everyone he met. He didn't have a real friend in the world. One day Dad made the statement to Marty, "I hate people!" Marty replied, "You don't really mean that." He answered, "Oh, yes I do!"

It was Dottie who pointed something out to Frank and Marty that had not occurred to them. What Dad was doing had nothing to do with love. It had to do with who would be there for him whenever he needed them. He had used his money as a weapon for years. The man didn't know a damn thing about love. He didn't care about anyone but himself. Dad was the king of control freaks. When Frank suggested that he leave everything to Marge and be done with it, Dad knew he had lost total control over his son.

Marty asked Dottie, "The next time you get on the subject of Dad with Uncle Frank, would you please ask him at what point in Dad's life did he become so full of hate and bitterness?" (Dad was eight years younger than Uncle Frank. He was born after their mother had lost two babies at birth and she spoiled him rotten.) Dottie asked her Dad and he said, "Mike's always been that way, even as a child. I'll never forget the day before our dear Mother went into the hospital for major surgery that took her life; she prepared dinner for us and Mike screamed at her, up one side and down the other, because she didn't cook it the way he liked it. I remember one time when Mike and Ann were first married and they got into a fight. Mike was taking off in the car and Ann tried to stop him. He came very close to running over her with the car, very close. You don't ever cross Mike! It doesn't matter who you are, you never cross him!"

A few months went by and they never heard from Dad or Marge, then Marge called one night. Marty thought something had happened to Dad from the look on Frank's face, but he wasn't saying much at all to Marge, he was just listening. When he hung up, Marty asked, "What is it, what happened?" He said, "Its Aunt Rose, she died." Marty tried to comfort Frank by saying, "I know its sad Frank, but she's in a better place. Her life has been hell for sometime, being almost blind and not able to hear. Dottie and Uncle Frank both told us that she was sleeping most of the time. It's really a blessing." Frank looked at her and said, "Not the way she went! Aunt Rose went out to help Uncle Frank put out the trash for pick-up tomorrow. He left the car on the street last night and didn't put it away in the garage. After they rolled out the barrels, he started to drive up that long driveway, and Aunt Rose was walking right in front of the car. He probably yelled at her to get out of the way and she didn't hear him. He told the police he hit the brake, and his foot slipped off of the brake and hit the gas pedal. He froze and the car took off, hitting Aunt Rose and dragging her for about a hundred feet. The garage door was shut and he drove right through it." Marty stood there looking at Frank in shock! She finally said, "Uncle Frank ran over Aunt Rose with the car and killed her?" Frank answered, "You got it!" Marty then said, "We've got to call Dottie. She must be a basket case! Uncle Frank will never survive this! He's probably going berserk! They called Dottie, but she couldn't talk. Her Dad was right there. She told them she would call them back the next day.

Frank called his Dad to tell him how sorry he was to hear about Aunt Rose. Dad still didn't want to talk to Frank, and hung up. Not even a horrible tragedy like this could soften this hardheaded bastard!

Dottie called back the next day and told them her Dad was staying at her house. He was resting at the time. She said, "Last night Mom and Dad's neighbor called me and told me what happened. I drove up to Arcadia immediately, and when I arrived; the place was crawling with police doing their investigation. Yellow tape was blocking off the scene of the accident. That long drive-way had Mom's blood and skin all over it. I'll never be able to forget what I saw on that drive-way. The whole neighborhood was standing around watching. The police questioned the neighbors, trying to find someone who actually saw what happened. Dad was sitting down, rubbing his bald head with his hands, and kept saying over and over, 'I killed my wife! My God! I killed my wife!'"

The police called it a homicide. They did not prosecute, but they did take Uncle Frank's driver's license. He was ninety-seven years old and Aunt Rose had just turned eighty-nine.

When Frank and Marty called Dottie the next day, she told them, "You won't believe what your Dad said to my Dad to comfort him, 'Oh, just forget about it!' Can you believe that? You run over and kill your wife of sixty-eight years and you're supposed to just forget about it!" After a couple of days, Uncle Frank insisted that Dottie take him home. Uncle Frank wanted Frank to be one of the pallbearers. Dad said, "No way!" When Dottie told Frank and Marty that, they knew they couldn't go back to California for the funeral. Dad obviously did not want them there. They felt their presence would make the circumstances that much more difficult for everyone. The police didn't release the body until they completed their investigation nine days later, so they couldn't have the funeral until ten days after the accident.

Six days after Aunt Rose died; Dad cornered Dottie on the driveway where her mother was killed. He asked Dottie, "Have you talked to Frank and Marty?" Dottie answered, "Of course! I talk to them all the time." Dad said, "Then you know what has been going on. You know it's my money and my decision on what to do with it. But if my son called me and apologized, I might change my will back to include him again." Dottie said simply, "I'm sorry, Uncle Mike, but what you are doing is not right. It's not fair." Dad yelled at her, "You're on their side! Let me tell you something! My son is a greedy money-hungry son of a bitch!" Dottie just walked off and left him. Frank told Dottie, "Even if I wanted to apologize, I don't even know what I would apologize for. I'm the one who told him to leave it all to Marge and be done with it. How does that make me the greedy one?"

Uncle Frank's health went down hill the following year and Dottie moved him in with her. He had cancer and became bedridden; wearing depends and living on Ensure. Marge called

Dottie to give her hell because Uncle Frank wasn't calling his brother every week! Dad would not pay for a long distance call to talk to his dying brother! After a couple of months, Uncle Frank couldn't talk and went into a semi-coma. He passed away two weeks later. This time, Frank did not call his Dad. He knew Dad would just refuse to talk to him again.

Mary, Frank's step-mother, was failing physically and losing it mentally. Dad had his son-in-law, Dick, call her kids to tell them, "Come get your mother. Dad can't take care of her." There was no way Dad was going to put her in a convalescent home and pay for it. Her kids told him they would come pick her up when he filed for divorce. Dad screamed at them, "I don't want any God damn divorce!" Dad and Mary were married for twenty-three years, but he just wanted to throw her out like a piece of garbage.

Mary went on a walk in the middle of the night, wearing just her nightgown. A nice man saw her and picked her up. She was able to give him directions to her daughter's home, but had lost it mentally. However, Mary knew she didn't want to see or talk to her husband and stayed with her daughter Eve.

When Mary's kids called Dad to make arrangements to pick up her things, they were informed they could only come when Marge was there. When they arrived and went into Mary's bedroom to pack, Marge stood over them to see everything they took. There wasn't one thing in that bedroom that didn't belong to Mary, including the furniture. When they wanted to take the bedroom furniture that Mary had before she even married Dad, he refused. He didn't want an empty room. Mary passed away a few months later. Dad didn't even buy flowers for his wife's grave, much less pay for the burial.

Marge finally has her Daddy all to herself now, but she is miserable. What goes around comes around, and Marge's world has crumbled down around her. Dick and Marge have lost friends and the people in their church refuse to work with them on projects. Dick is going on camping trips twice a year for three months at a time, without Marge, traveling across the country. He buys the cheap whiskey now and drinks more than ever. Dad can not drive anymore, so Marge drives him to his appointments and runs his errands. He's in trouble with the IRS for back taxes—there goes a lot of Marge's inheritance. What a shame, after she worked so hard for so many years to get it all.

CHAPTER FORTY-SEVEN

Marty still spent two hours or more on the phone with her sister every Sunday. Laura used to be such a fussy housekeeper and had become exactly like Dad. Dad was the king of pack rats and now, Laura is the queen of pack rats. Actually, she has become a junk dealer and her son, Roy is her business partner. They go to yard sales to buy junk and then fix it up to sell at the flea market. Frank and Marty refer to them as *Sanford and Son*. Laura talked constantly to Marty about how badly she needed to weed things out, but would keep right on buying more and more junk. Marty repeatedly asked her not to talk about her prize purchases and treasures, that it gave her nightmares about growing up surrounded with all of Dad's junk, but she just kept going on and on about it.

Marty's brother, Byron suffered a stroke and was flown to the hospital in Wichita. A couple of days later, he had brain surgery. It was very serious, but it did not affect his speech. He had to relearn how to swallow and also had extensive therapy to regain his coordination on his right side. It was a long road back, but he made a fantastic recovery. Brent and Faith went to Wichita every weekend to see Byron until they moved him to a convalescent home in Springfield, Missouri where they lived. Marty sent a check to Brent and Faith for five hundred dollars to help them with their extra expenses. After ten days without hearing from them, Marty called them and Faith answered the phone. Faith said they had been sick for two days. Marty asked, "Have you been too sick to get your mail?" Faith answered as you would say to someone who just gave you a two-cent tip, "No, we got it, thanks." Brent never did acknowledge it, much less thank her. When Marty got Brent on the phone a week later, he said he was too tired to talk.

Byron was able to go home to Larned again after two months in the convalescent hospital in Springfield and was doing great. He retired and his income increased by fifty percent with three different pension checks each month. He bought a small brick house up on snob hill. After hearing about him being on snob hill a hundred times on the phone, Frank and Marty kidded him that he didn't need help if he could live on snob hill. So he started putting on his poor act again because he wanted to come to Vegas and expected them to pay for it. Marty told him if he paid for his hotel and plane ticket they would pay for everything else.

Marty swore they wouldn't kill themselves and spend a fortune on him again to show him a good time in Vegas. The last time he came, they went to the Lagoon Saloon one night and there were no empty tables. Marty saw a man sitting by himself and asked him if they could join him. He said, "Sure!" They ordered their drinks and Frank paid for them, as usual. In the course of conversation, the guy told them about properties he had all over the world. After walking out of the saloon, Byron said in a very angry tone, "That guy should have paid for our drinks!" Marty asked, "Why?" Byron replied, "Because he could have paid for them and never missed the money!" Marty was appalled and said, "What has that got to do with it! He has never seen us before and will never see us again! Why in the hell should he buy us drinks! It was nice of him to let us sit with him. If anything, we should have bought him one!"

After Byron had his stroke, Marty thought he would have a different attitude since he experienced the kiss of death. Oh, his attitude changed all right, but for the worse! No matter how hard they tried, Byron had a way about him that made them feel they never did enough for him. He acted like Frank and Marty had a money tree that produced upon command.

When Byron arrived, they picked him up at the airport. As they walked to their car; he held his arms up in the air and leaned forward, making it look like it was such an effort to walk.

Marty saw right through him. He had already slipped once on the phone, telling her about one day when he was walking from the car into the cafe to eat lunch. It started raining, so he ran to the door. He said, "Then I limped in like I'm supposed to." Marty knew what buttons to push because he had an ego as big as all outdoors. She said, "You wouldn't get so tired if you put your arms down and straightened up your back. The way you are walking, you look like a ninety year old man." Byron immediately put his arms down, straightened up his back and walked normally! Frank and Marty couldn't keep up with him!

They went to the Mandalay Bay Casino Hotel for dinner in their lovely café. Byron pulled out his cell phone to call Aunt Lula. He really loved playing the big man since he moved to snob hill. His head had blown up like a hot air balloon!

Marty told Byron on the phone before coming that he needed to wear good supporting sneakers that were very comfortable. He said he had sneakers that were not anything to look at, but they would clean up and be fine. Marty said she would take him to the outlet store where Frank gets his sneakers to buy some new ones. Byron came out to Vegas wearing a pair of sneakers so broken down they were not good enough to give to a bum on the street. Byron asked when they were going to the outlet to buy his shoes and they took him down that day. As he was trying them on, he turned to Frank and asked, "You are going to let me pay for my shoes, aren't you?" Frank answered, "Yes". Byron got so mad; he was red in the face! Marty thought he was going to throw the shoes across the store the way he was slamming the shoe boxes around! Frank and Marty just ignored the whole thing and proceeded to show him the town.

They treated him to a luscious breakfast at the Ceres Restaurant, surrounded with a beautiful tropical garden with brooks and waterfalls, in the J.W. Marriot Hotel. The Rampart Casino, in the same location, is Frank and Marty's second home and they eat at their great Promenade Café all the time. They took Byron there to give him a taste of the local life. He stayed in a lovely upper deluxe room at the Suncoast Casino Hotel, down the street from the Rampart. They went to the elegant buffet at the Golden Nugget Casino and enjoyed the Fremont Experience, then to the breathtaking Bellagio to see the dancing fountain show on their eight acre lake. The fantastic buffet in the Green Valley Ranch Casino was Byron's favorite meal of the week. In the Venetian, they took a stroll along Venice's Grand Canal to St. Mark's Square where they had Italian Opera singers performing in beautiful costumes. Afterwards, they dined at the Grand Lux Café. Of course, they had to sip pinacoladas at the Lagoon Saloon in the Mirage by the rain forest. Later, they walked through the beautiful Desert Passage in the Aladdin. They took a leisurely drive through the Red Rock Canyon that was beautiful and green from recent rains. The wild flowers were in bloom.

After four days, Frank could barely walk. His bad foot and knee were killing him. Marty's back was hurting and she was having splitting headaches. However! Byron was still going strong—like the Duracell bunny! On the fifth day, Marty got out of bed and her heart kicked-in doing its thing of rapid heart beat, called tachycardia. She was on medication for it daily, but with over doing, being totally stressed out with Byron's attitude, plus not getting her rest, it took off in high speed. She took an extra heart pill and repeatedly did her exercise of holding her breath for as long as she could while bearing down, but it took a couple of hours to get it to slow down. After Marty has one of these episodes, she is wiped out for days. The doctor explained to her, it's just like being on the treadmill for several hours.

It was Byron's last day. Frank went over to check Byron out of the hotel; took him to breakfast in the Suncoast Sienna Café, and brought him back to the house. Byron was furious that they were not going anywhere that day. He showed no concern whatsoever for Frank's leg or Marty's heart. He was acting like a total ass, being very sarcastic. Marty sat there looking at him and thought, "This is my brother who I have coddled and protected all of my life! He really doesn't give a shit about us! He only cares about what we can do *for* him!" Marty's eyes were suddenly wide open where it concerned her brother. She screamed at him, "I don't think you have a clue on how I feel! What's more, you don't give a damn!" Mary Lou, their dear friend next door, was upset over Byron's attitude and told Marty, "Call the airport service to take him to the airport. Neither one of you are in any shape to drive him!" Marty called and paid for it herself like they did everything else. They sent a polished chauffeur dressed for the Queen of England in a beautiful black Lincoln Town Car. As the chauffeur loaded up his luggage, Byron and Marty managed to say a civil good-bye. After they turned the corner and were out of sight, Frank waved his arms and yelled, "Hallelujah!" Then he turned to Marty and said, "I don't ever want him back here again!" Marty replied, "You got that right!"

After Byron got home, he called to let them know he arrived safely. Before the trip, he was calling three to five times every week, talking from one to two hours each phone call, about absolutely nothing. He had a service plan on his phone for unlimited calls for a flat monthly fee. The day after Byron returned home, Marty let her answering machine pick up all of her calls. Then he started calling four times every day, harassing her to death!

Marty said to Frank, "I have really had it with Byron and Laura ruining our lives with their phone calls. Why are we putting up with this? I'm changing our phone number and it will be unlisted!" Frank said, "Its fine with me!" Marty called the phone company and they had a new number the next day. She notified all of their friends and anyone else who needed their new phone number.

A week later, they received a note from Byron and a letter from Laura asking Marty to call them, but didn't say anything to indicate they got the message. *Their elevators were not going to the top floor.*

Within two weeks, Marty quit having her nightmares! Her back and neck were not killing her! The severe headaches were gone! She couldn't believe how much better she felt! Even her stomach was doing much better. She didn't have to take tums constantly. Frank's bad foot and knee were doing better. He had to stay off of his feet as much as possible for a couple of weeks after Byron left and did extra exercises his therapist showed him at the gym.

Frank and Marty were relaxed; joking and laughing again! Marty said to Frank, "This is great! Why didn't I do this a long time ago? We have our own little family here, our friends and neighbors!"

It's been over four years now, since Frank and Marty were dejected by Frank's family. However, after they made the adjustment of not having family in their lives and had time to heal from being so deeply hurt; Frank and Marty realized just how great it is—not dealing with all of their constant insults, criticism, lies, rudeness and total lack of consideration!

On the beautiful day of realization, when it finally dawned on them just how fantastic their life had become—Marty walked into the living room with a smile on her face and asked Frank in a whisper, "Listen! Do you hear that?" Frank smiled and answered in a whisper, "Hear what?" Marty said as if she was making an announcement to the whole world, "**PEACE! LISTEN TO ALL THAT PEACE! WE ARE FREE AT LAST!**"

About the Author

After growing up in Kansas, Marty Wurtz's independent spirit led her to Denver and then to Southern California to follow her dreams. The greater part of her professional career was spent as an accountant and business order writer with large corporations. Her passion was constant projects and lavish improvements on every home she shared with her husband and their poodles, selling each home for a large profit. As an avid bridge player, she served as Bridge Chairman for a variety of bridge clubs for nearly twenty years. When her husband retired in 1997, they moved to fabulous Las Vegas, Nevada.